UPSHUR COUNTY, WEST VIRGINIA:

ABSTRACTS OF WILLS,

1851-1884

Originally prepared by:

The West Virginia Historical Records Survey
Work Projects Administration (WPA)
1941

JANAWAY PUBLISHING
2012

Upshur County West Virginia:
Abstracts of Wills, 1851-1884

Originally prepared by:
The Work Project Administration (WPA)
1941

Reprinted by:

Janaway Publishing, Inc.
732 Kelsey Ct.
Santa Maria, CA 93454
(805) 925-1038
www.JanawayGenealogy.com

2006, 2012

ISBN: 978-1-59641-274-3

Made in the United States of America

CALENDAR OF WILLS IN WEST VIRGINIA

NO. 49.   UPSHUR COUNTY
(Buckhannon)

Prepared by

The West Virginia Historical Records Survey
Division of Community Service Programs
Work Projects Administration

Charleston, West Virginia
The West Virginia Historical Records Survey
August   1941

UPSHUR COUNTY, WEST VIRGINIA

Historical Records Survey Projects

> Sargent B. Child, Director
> Eva Margaret Carnes, State Supervisor

Research and Records Programs

> Harvey E. Becknell, Director
> George W. Hubley, Jr., Regional Supervisor
> Paul B. Shanks, State Supervisor

Division of Community Service Programs

> Florence Kerr, Assistant Commissioner
> Mary G. Moon, Chief Regional Supervisor
> Irene Gillooly, State Director

WORK PROJECTS ADMINISTRATION

> Howard O. Hunter, Commissioner
> George H. Field, Regional Director
> J. N. Alderson, State Administrator

✻ ✻ ✻ ✻ ✻ ✻ ✻

Sponsor: West Virginia Department of Archives and History

Co-sponsor: The County Court of Upshur County

ABSTRACTS OF WILLS, 1851-1884

PREFACE

The Historical Records Survey was established in West Virginia in 1936 as a part of the Federal Historical Records Survey, under the national direction of Dr. Luther H. Evans. Pursuant to an Act of Congress the Federal Historical Records Survey, with other Work Projects Administration federal projects, was terminated August 31, 1939; its work in West Virginia has been continued since then by the West Virginia Historical Records Survey, sponsored by the West Virginia Department of Education until July 1, 1940 and after that date by the West Virginia Department of Archives and History. Mr. Sargent B. Child succeeded Dr. Evans as Director of Historical Records Survey Projects March 1, 1940. Up to the present time the Survey throughout the nation has issued approximately 1,315 publications.

The volume here presented is the first of a series of calendars of wills which will be prepared and published by the West Virginia Historical Records Survey from the recorded wills of the 55 counties in our State. It is hoped that the abstracts of this series will present a picture of the persons who resided in the county prior to 1885 and of the property which they owned. Later series of publications will supplement this information by listing appraisements and bills of sale.

The Record of Wills series in each county have been carefully abstracted by the county worker and rechecked by the State editorial staff. Proper names and descriptions of property are spelled as they appear in the recordings. The entries are entered chronologically by date of probate and are arranged as follows: name of testator, occupation of testator if shown, place will made, date will made, date of probate, names of devisees, name of executor, abstract of will, names of witnesses to will, book and page number of recording, and assigned calendar number. Abbreviations are used whenever permissable in order to shorten the abstracts. Because of the frequent use of names in boundary descriptions, names of legatees are set out in solid caps in order to avoid confusion.

Initial work on this volume was done by Mrs. Beatrice Arnold Giffin and Miss Ruth Hawkins of Buckhannon. Compilation of entries and rechecking was done by the State editorial staff under the direction of John M. Carr, assistant project technician.

Acknowledgment of assistance is given to Allen B. Cutright, clerk of the county court of Upshur County, for the advice and help which he gave to Mrs. Giffin throughout the abstracting of the wills. Acknowledgment is also made to the County Court of Upshur County, co-sponsor of the project, for their cooperation and contributions.

Appreciation is also expressed to Joseph N. Alderson, State Director of Work Projects Administration, Mrs. Irene Fallon Gillooly, Director of Community Service Programs, and Paul B. Shanks, State Supervisor of Research and Records Programs, for their kind cooperation in administration of the project.

A list of completed publications of the Historical Records Survey in West Virginia will be found in the back of this volume. Requests for information concerning these publications should be addressed to the Historical Records Survey, 210 Smallridge Building, Quarrier Street, Charleston, W. Va.

EVA MARGARET CARNES
State Supervisor
The West Virginia Historical
Records Survey

Charleston, West Virginia
August 5, 1941

ABSTRACTS OF WILLS, 1851-1884

INTRODUCTION

Wills have long been of interest to genealogists because of the many names appearing therein and the definite relationships usually set forth in the distribution of the testator's accumulated property. From the standpoint of social history they may be considered equally valuable because we find listed here much of the property owned by the testator and special emphasis is usually placed on what he considered the most valuable of his possessions. The studious man carefully disposes of his library, the cattle dealer gives his best stock to his favored son or daughter, the agriculturist definitely defines his land ownership and sometimes even specifies the crops which shall be planted, the store owner describes his property and the contents of his store. The industrial life of the county is reflected in the wills as property ownership indicates change of investments. Upshur County Wills show the development of the agricultural pursuits of the county, the purchase or the acquiring of free land as it was opened throughout the west, and the development of towns and town property.

Upshur County's will records are complete from 1851, the date of establishment of the county. In compiling the calendar it has been deemed wise to limit the publication to wills recorded prior to 1885. Thus only Will Book A has been used. These records will be found in the office of the Clerk of the County Court.

Wills in West Virginia are probated in the county court,[1] whose jurisdiction is exclusive and original in all matter of probate, appointment and qualification of personal representatives, and the settlement of their accounts. The will is presented to the court in regular session by the executor, if an executor has been named, who makes oath that to his best knowledge and belief the will is the last testament of the decedent. The oath is attached to the will and the order of probate and recording is issued by the court.[2] The executor then gives bond to the court for the faithful performance of his duties.[3] At the time of the qualification of the personal representative he is required to present to the court, or to the clerk

---

1. W. Va. Const., 1872, ch. 24, art. 8.
2. Va. Code, 1849, ch. 30, art. 3; ibid., 1860, ch. 130, art. 3; W. Va. Code, 1868, ch. 85, art. 3; W. Va. Acts, 1872-73, ch. 122, art. 3; Code, 1923, ch. 85, art. 3.
3. Va. Code, 1849, ch. 130, art. 5; ibid., 1860, ch. 130, art. 5; W. Va. Code, 1868, ch. 85, art. 5; W. Va. Acts, 1872-73, ch. 122, art. 5; ibid., 1903, ch. 13, art. 5; ibid., 1907, ch. 56, art. 5; Code, 1923, ch. 85, art. 5.

UPSHUR COUNTY, WEST VIRGINIA

Introduction vi

thereof who acts in vacation of the court, a list of all heirs of the estate, together with their addresses and relationship to the testator[1] and the list is recorded.

Following the qualification of the personal representative the county court refers the estate to a commissioner of accounts who acts as an agent for the body, examines and approves all reports of the executor or administrator, determines the amounts of distribution, accepts claims against the estate, makes reports to the court of all matters in the estate, and in general relieves the court.[2] The court, or the clerk in vacation, then appoints not less than three or more than five persons to appraise all real and personal property in the estate and an equal number in any other county or counties in which property is owned. The appraisers so named, after having taken oath, list and appraise all property held in the estate and present the list, which is signed by them, to the commissioner of accounts to whom the estate has been referred and who examines the list, presents one copy to the clerk of the county court for recording and sends one copy to the Tax Commissioner of West Virginia.[3]

Within two months after qualification the personal representative presents to the commissioner of accounts an inventory of all property received by him to be administered, the list being prepared in duplicate and setting forth a full description and the location of all property.[4] The commissioner examines this inventory and presents it to the county court for approval and recording. Within two months after the sale of any property in the estate the personal representative is required to make an accounting of such sale to the commission-

---

1. W. Va. Acts, 1903, ch. 13, art. 5; ibid., 1907, ch. 56, arts. 1, 5; W. Va. Code, 1923, ch. 85, arts. 1, 5.
2. W. Va. Acts, 1863, ch. 36, art. 1; ibid., 1882, ch. 68, art. 6; ibid., 1883, ch. 28, art. 6; ibid., 1885, ch. 26, art. 6; W. Va. Code, 1923, ch. 87, art. 6; W. Va. Acts, 1933, Ex. Sess., ch. 57.
3. Va. Code, 1849, ch. 130, art. 12; ibid., 1860, ch. 130, art. 12; W. Va. Code, 1868, ch. 85, art. 12; W. Va. Acts, 1872-73, ch. 122, art. 12; ibid., 1904, ch. 7, art. 12; ibid., 1907, ch. 56, art. 12; W. Va. Code, 1923, ch. 85, art. 12; W. Va. Acts, 1937, ch. 66.
4. Va. Code, 1849, ch. 132, art. 3; ibid., 1860, ch. 132, art. 3; W. Va. Code, 1868, ch. 87, art. 2; W. Va. Acts, 1872-73, ch. 234; ibid., 1882, ch. 68, art. 2; W. Va. Code, 1923, ch. 87, art. 2; W. Va. Acts, 1937, ch. 64.

er of accounts together with the proof thereof and after exam-
ination by the commissioner and approval of the court the
account is recorded.[1]

Annual accountings are made to the commissioner by the
fiduciary of all receipts and disbursements of funds in the
estate[2] except in the case of small estates in which an accounting may be required only once in three years.[3] After the payment of all claims and settlement of all debts against the estate the fiduciary makes report to the commissioner as a final
settlement which the commissioner in turn reports to the county court. The court then issues an order for the payment of
legacies and the distribution of all funds remaining in the
estate.[4]

Additional information relating to estates in this volume
such as bills of sale, appraisements, and settlements, may be
obtained from the records of the clerk of the county court of
Upshur County.

JOHN MERRILL CARR
Assistant Project Technician

1. Va. Code, 1849, ch. 132, art. 4; ibid., 1860, ch. 132,
   art. 4; W. Va. Code, 1868, ch. 87, art. 3; W. Va. Acts,
   1872-73, ch. 234, art. 4; ibid., 1882, ch. 68, art. 3;
   W. Va. Code, 1923, ch. 87, art. 3.
2. Va. Code, 1849, ch. 132, art. 7; ibid., 1860, ch. 132,
   art. 7; W. Va. Code, 1868, ch. 87, art. 6; W. Va. Acts,
   1872-73, ch. 234, art. 7; ibid., 1882, ch. 68, art. 6;
   ibid., 1885, ch. 26, art. 6; W. Va. Code, 1923, ch. 87,
   art. 6.
3. Ibid.
4. W. Va. Code, Michie, 1937, sec. 4170.

ABSTRACTS OF WILLS, 1851-1884

ABBREVIATIONS

a.	acre
ackn.	acknowledged
afsd.	aforesaid
Bk.	Book
bro(s).	brother(s)
dau(s).	daughter(s)
etc.	and so forth
ex(s).	executor(s)
grdau(s).	granddaughter(s)
j.p.	justice of the peace
mos.	months
n.d.	not dated
n.p.	notary public
nr.	near
p.	page
pd.	paid
pmt(s).	payment(s)
pp.	pages
pvt.	private
sd.	said
teste.	testated
tshp.	township
Va.	Virginia
Va. Vol. Inf.	Virginia Volunteer Infantry
W. Va.	West Virginia
yr(s).	year(s)

ABSTRACTS OF WILLS, 1851-1884

CALENDAR OF WILLS UPSHUR COUNTY

(1, 2)

WOOD, JOSEPH, farmer, Upshur County, Va., n.d.; June
term, 1851.
L.L.D.Loudin, ex.
Testator desires pmt. of debts and funeral expenses from
first money pd. to ex. from accounts, if funds insufficient
enough property to be sold; slaves to remain "on farm" until
youngest child (not named) becomes of age then to be equally
divided among "all my children"; widow to retain her 1/3 interest during life, at her death her share to be sold and proceeds to be divided among children; household and kitchen furniture and other necessary personalty to remain on farm; farm
to be kept in use of family until youngest child reaches legal
age then to be sold with reservation of dwelling house and 1/3
of realty to wife for life use; remainder to be equally divided
among children and at widow's death same division to be made.
Teste., Mary F. Rothwell, Jac. Waugh, J. B. Shreve.
Bk. 1, pp. 1, 2. /1/

JACK, JACOB, Upshur County, Va., 3 Jan. 1852; Feb. term,
1852.
Wife EASTER, sons, JONATHAN S. JACK, HENRY M. JACK, JOHN
S. JACK, daus., SARAH S. SIMS, NANCY JANE BURR, ANGELINA JACK,
EASTER S. JACK, ANDSON R. JACK, HENDERSON JACK. Wife Easter,
ex.
Testator desires pmt. of debts and funeral expenses; bequeaths to son JONATHAN S. JACK, 109¼ a. tract of land on
which sd. son resides; to son HENRY M. JACK, 100 a. adjoining
afsd. bequest; to son JOHN S. JACK, $50; to dau. SARAH S. SIMS,
$50 to be pd. in 5 yrs. after date of will; to dau. NANCY JANE
BURR, $10 to be pd. in 5 yrs. after date of will; to wife
EASTER remainder of personalty and realty for use during life-
time and at her death to be divided equally among "four children living at home" ANGELINA JACK, EASTER S. JACK, ANSON R.
JACK and HENDERSON JACK.
Teste., David Bennett, Aaron Gould, Jonathan Hefaner.
Bk. A, p. 3. /2/

HYRE, PETER, Upshur County, Va., 8 Jan. 1852; Feb. term,
1852.
Wife, ELIZABETH, sons ELMORE HYRE, JOHN HYRE, TURNER
HYRE, STEWART HYRE, HENRY HYRE, TAYLOR HYRE, daus. RUHANNAH
SIMMONS, MINNIE /HYRE/. Son Elmore Hyre, ex.
Testator bequeaths to wife ELIZABETH, "sorrel mare and
young black horse," 4 cows, 15 sheep, 7 hogs, 2 yoke of oxen,
farming equipment to carry on farm, all household furniture
"except a good bed to each of the girls" use of farm for widowhood; to dau. RHUHANNAH SIMMONS, prior gifts consisting of
cow, calf, 3 sheep, one side saddle, bed clothes, valued at
$38; to son ELMORE HYRE, horse and saddle valued at $100 and
100 a. tract on Beaver Run where sd. Elmore resides, ex. to
make deed with provision that he pay $70, prior pmts. having

amounted to $30, pmt. to be made to "Turner and the rest of
the boys younger than he when they are of age"; to son JOHN
HYRE, prior gift of horse and saddle and cow valued at $100,
and also 100 a. tract on Left Hand Fork of Bulls Run where sd.
John now resides with provision that he pay $100 as in afsd.
bequest; to son TURNER HYRE, prior gift of one young bay mare
and saddle; to son STEWARD HYRE, "my dun mare's youngest colt";
to HENRY and TAYLOR, "colts or horses equal to Turner and
Steward"; to dau. MINNIE, "sorrells youngest colt"; remainder
of realty and personalty to wife ELIZABETH.
    Teste., Pascal P. Young, Benjamin Gould, William S. Bready.
Bk. A, pp. 4, 5.   /3/

    JACKSON, HENRY, Upshur County, Va., 20 Nov. 1848; Mar.
term, 1852.
    Wife, ELIZABETH, son, EDWARD C. JACKSON, daus. ELISABESS
P. PREBBELL, AMANDA M. PREBBEL, RACHEL C. MILLER, MARY S.M.
ROSA WYRICK, children, DECATURE, SAMUEL, DEXTOR, JAMES ALONZO,
MARRION ORLANDO, MELISSA, GEORGE WASHINGTON, ARTEMISHA,
GALIPSO MERO. Wife, Elizabeth Jackson, ex.
    Testator bequeaths as follows "I have given unto my sons
by the first wife all that I intend to or can except EDWARD
C. JACKSON. I give to my three daughters ELISABESS P.
PREBBELL, AMANDA M. PREBBEL, RACHEL C. MILLER the land that
John Cozad let me have known as Crutslow Bend to be sold at
one, two and three year payments for AMANDA M. PREBBELL to
have one halfe and the other to be divided between other two
daughters, To my son EDWARD the land promised to me by John B.
Shrev and Henry O. Middleton where Benjamin Miller lives, a
cow worth Twelve dollards, a Horse and saddle worth Fortyfive
dollars but the one hundred acres is not conved Middleton and
Shrev for him to have two hundred dollars mony, Notes or land.
The land or money to be on intrest for him as he is not of
sound mind...He has pat of land that his mother owned that is
to be on interest to support him. To my daughter MARY S.M.
ROSA WYRICK fifty dollars when there is so mutch of the land
soald to pay her without pressing on my wife, One cow one saddle
worth thirty doles. To my wife ELIZABETH as long as she is my
widow the whole of my land and moveable property not otherwise
disposed of for Shool and board and raise my children on that
she is the mother of, to wit: DECATURE, SAMUEL, DEXTOR, JAMES
ALONZO, MARRION ORLANDO, MELISSA, GEORGE WASHINGTON, ARTEMISHA,
GALISPO MERO as she may think best but she must sell that worth-
less Negro garlo if she is not sold in my time also I have several law suits now pending and if I go out of time before they
are desided, then suites to be renewed in the names if my last
wife's children. School the children if possible, If any of
my children or wife after my death shall dispute my right to
dispose of foregoing property they shall be cut off from all
that is devised to them that it shall be divised to the last
wife's children"; states that foregoing will is "wholy in my
own handwrite."
    Teste., James T. Hartman, David Hall, Robert Johnson, John
B. Shreve.
    Bk. A, pp. 5-7.   /4/

ABBOTT, DANIEL, Upshur County, Va., 17 May, 1853; June
term, 1853.
   Mother, FRANCIS ABBOTT, bro. JOHN W. ABBOTT, bro.-in-law,
ROBERT PRITT. John D. Simin, ex.
   Testator desires pmt. of debts and funeral expenses; bequeaths to mother FRANCIS ABBOTT, $10; remainder of property
to bro. JOHN W. ABBOTT and bro.-in-law ROBERT PRITT to be
equally divided, sd. JOHN W. ABBOTT to have "my rifle gun,"
sd. ROBERT PRITT to have "new gun."
   Teste., A. W. C. Lemmons, David E. Casto.
   Bk. A, p. 8.   /5/

FRETWELL, SARAH J., Upshur County, Va., 10 Mar. 1853;
May term, 1854.
   Son, SAMUEL B. FRETWELL, other children not named.   Son,
Samuel B. Fretwell, ex.
   Testatrix desires pmt. of debts from personalty; bequeaths
to son SAMUEL B. FRETWELL a negro boy named William "for his
services in support of my family and the education of my infant children"; if sd. Samuel die without lawful issue, sd.
William to be sold and proceeds thereof to be divided among
surviving children of testatrix; devises that "the four slaves
and the future increase of the females should pass and go in
fee simple" by deed on record in Albemarl, Lewis, and Upshur
Counties, sd. slaves to be kept together until testatrix's
youngest child becomes of legal age, then executor to sell
slaves and distribute proceeds equally among children, or make
equal division of the slaves; remainder of realty and personalty to be distributed as preceding bequest.
   Teste., Henry Ours, M. Y. Humphery, R. Fretwell.
   Bk. A, pp. 10, 11.   /6/

STRADER, JONAS, Upshur County, Va., 8 April 1854; May
term, 1854.
   Wife and children, not named. Bro., Valentine Strader,
ex.
   Testator desires ex. to sell "the tract of land purchased
of Hinkle and that portion of the home place lying on the
southeast side over the hill be both sold after my death. My
cattle is to be pastured on my lands and to be sold in the fall,
also, the McCan horse after the planting, all bonds coming to
me or debts to be collected and debts paid"; bequeaths remainder of personalty to wife for widowhood and to children (not
named); desires that ex. contract with Jacob B. Strader "or
some other workman" to build and finish a house 26' x 16' for
wife and children; bequeaths to wife "as many milch cows and
heifers as she desires."
   Teste., D. S. Haselden, D. S. Pinnell, James E. Slaughter.
   Bk. A, pp. 9, 10.   /7/

MAYO, NANCY H., Upshur County, Va., 29 Apr. 1854; July term, 1854.
TASVILL MARSHALL, CLAUDIUS B. MAYO, MALINDA HURNDON, ANN E. DURETT, SOPHIA MARSHALL, (relationship not shown). Tasvill Marshall, ex.
Testatrix bequeaths to TASVILL MARSHALL, $100; to CLAUDIUS B. MAYO, MALINDA HURNDON, ANN E. DURETT, and SOPHIA MARSHALL equal division of all money, bonds or other personalty.
Teste., Claudius B. Mayo, Valentine H. Dicenson, Mary E. Haris.
Bk. A, p. 17.   /8/

GIBSON, ALEXANDER I., Upshur County, Va., 14 Oct. 1854; Nov. term, 1854.
Sister COLUMBIA A. GIBSON, bro. CHARLES W. GIBSON, step-mother MARGARET GIBSON, children of sister CAROLINE LAWHORN. Father, Enoch Gibson, ex.
Testator bequeaths "Whereas my grandfather the late John Jackson in his bequests give unto my later mother Elizabeth Gibson who was Elizabeth Jackson a certain tract or parcel of land now lying in the county of Upshur and in the possession of my father Enoch Gibson which will descend to the lawful heirs of her body in fee simple" sd. land to be divided into 3 equal parts, one part to sister COLUMBIA A. GIBSON, and two parts to bro. CHARLES W. GIBSON when they reach legal age; if either of afsd. devisees die property to survivor, if both die one share in fee simple to testator's step mother MARGARET GIBSON, other share to remain in executor's hands for education and support of children of testator's sister CAROLINE LAWHORN; sister COLUMBIA A. GIBSON and bro. CHARLES W. GIBSON, to be educated as part of bequest to them.
Teste., Henry Ours, R. Fretwell.
Bk. A, pp. 18, 19.   /9/

POST, ABRAHAM, Upshur County, Va., 22 June 1854; March term, 1855.
Wife, CHRISTENA, sons ABRAM, DANIEL, ISAAC, GEORGE, daus. FANNY RADABAUGH, BARBARA SWECKER, MARY BENNETT, grdaus. CAROLINE ROHRBOUGH, ELIZABETH ROHRBOUGH, MARGARET LINCH, GEMIMAH CLARK, Sons, Abram Post and Daniel Post, exs.
Testator desires pmt. of debts and funeral expenses; queaths to wife CHRISTENA, "sufficient sum of money to maintain her comfortably for life to be paid by executors each year or when demanded by her not to exceed one hundred dollars each year"; exs. to collect all debts and sell all property except "my two-horse wagon and blacksmith tools"; to son ABRAM, sd. wagon and tools; to son ISAAC, in addition to prior gifts, $50; to son GEORGE, in addition to prior gifts, $50; to dau. FANNY, wife of Benjamin RADABAUGH, in addition to prior gifts, $50; to dau. BARBARA, wife of Daniel SWECKER, in addition to prior gifts, $20; to dau. MARY, wife of Simon BENNETT, $400; to grdau. CAROLINE ROHRBOUGH, $50; to grdau. ELIZABETH ROHRBOUGH

$50; to grdau. JEMIMAH, wife of Reiley CLARK, $50; to grdau.
MARGARET, wife of Daniel LINCH, $50; remainder of estate to
sons ABRAM and DANIEL POST.
Teste., G. W. Berlin, Fred'k. Berlin, H. McFaddin.
Bk. A, pp. 20-22.   /10/
Codicil: 8 Feb. 1855.
Testator bequeaths to grdau. GEMIMA CLARK, $300 to be in-
vested in land as follows: son Daniel Post is indebted to
testator for $400 of which he is to pay $300 for a tract of
land to be selected by Riley Clark, husband of sd. Gemima, deed
to be made in Gemima's name; to son DANIEL POST, remainder of
$400 note.
Teste., Jac. Waugh, Ira Post.

SEE, A/NTHONY/ B., Upshur County, Va., 30 June, 1855; July
term, 1855.
Wife JULIA, son RANDOLPH. Ezekeal Townsent and William
Townsent, exs.
Testator desires pmt. of debts and funeral expenses from
sale of homestead in French Creek and of stock; to wife JULIA
and son RANDOLPH, tract of land known as John Burr farm with
provision that they care for rest of children, not named; to
wife JULIA all household and kitchen furniture and farming
equipment.
Teste., Amos Brooks, John Shobe.
Bk. A, p. 25.   /11/

BROWNING, WILLIAM H., Upshur County, Va., 17 March 1856;
April term, 1856.
Wife MARY, children SARAH JANE, JULERATTA, JOHN WESLEY,
MARY SUSAN, GREENBEERY FULTON, JAMES HOPKINS. Wife, Mary, ex.
Testator bequeaths to wife MARY, choice of 2 negroes,
homestead to use as she pleases; after death of sd. Mary prop-
erty to be sold and divided equally among children SARAH JANE,
JULERATTA, JOHN WESLEY, MARY SUSAN, GREENBERRY FULTON, and
JAMES HOPKINS; remainder of personalty to be sold and used for
pmt. of debts; any residue of afsd. sale to be used for care
and education of children; executrix to give deed to James
Matheny for moiety for which he holds testator's title bond
"with all the purchase money paid on it."
Teste., M. Boatwright, D. H. Shumaker.
Bk. A, p. 23.   /12/

HAMNER, THOMAS, Upshur County, Va., 10 Apr., 1856; May
term, 1856.
Wife MARIA B. HAMNER, children not named. Wife Maria, ex.
Testator desires pmt. of debts and funeral expenses; to
wife MARIA B., all personalty and realty for life; at death of
sd. Maria property to be sold and equally divided among testa-
tor's children, not named.
Teste., Nathanial Moon Jr., Schuyler T. Moon, Nathaniel
Moon Sr., Nathanial H. Hannah, William G. Harlin.
Bk. A, p. 24.   /13/

GOULD, NATHAN, Upshur County, Va., 31 July, 1855; Oct. term, 1856.
Wife CEMANTHA, sons, JOSEPH, JOEL FREEMAN, NATHAN, JONATHAN, WATSON, JOSEPH, daus. ESTHER PHILLIPS, CELIA, ROXANA, CYNTHA ANN HOWES, MARTHA RICE, ELIZABETH BUTTON, JULIA CURTIS and LYDIA BROWN. No ex. named.
Testator bequeaths to son JOSEPH, all personalty with exception of household furniture and all realty with exception of 100 a. (testator's homestead) with provision that he care for testator's wife CEMANTHA for lifetime; also that sd. Joseph allow testator's sons JONATHAN and WATSON to reside with him, and work for him, until they reach legal age; should Joseph fail to support sd. Cemantha then realty and personalty to her for lifetime or widowhood; to wife CEMANTHA, all household furniture; to son JONATHAN 1/3 of remaining realty with provision that he pay testator's dau. ROXANNA $15; to son WATSON, 1/3 of realty with provision that he pay testator's dau. CELIA, $15; to son MARSHALL, prior gift of 50 a., on French Creek with provision that he pay testator's dau. ESTHER PHILLIPS, $15; son JOSEPH to pay testator's dau. CYNTHIA ANN HOWES, $15; to daus. ROXANNA and CELIA, same amount of household articles as "sisteres Esther and Cyntha Ann have"; to sons JOEL FREEMAN, and NATHAN, $1 each; to daus: MARTHA RICE, ELIZABETH BUTTON, JULIA CURTIS, and LYDIA BROWN, $1 each.
Teste., Anson Young, John Howes, Daniel Howes.
Bk. A, p. 26.   /14/

BROWNING, MARY, Upshur County, Va., 11 Nov., 1857; Dec. term, 1857.
Dau. SARAH JANE BROWNING, other children not named. Executor not named.
Testatrix bequeaths to eldest dau. SARAH JANE BROWNING, two servants George and Joseph, and a grey horse; remainder of household furniture, farm equipment, and stock to be sold and divided equally among all children, not named; for minor children money to be placed on interest and applied toward education until they reach legal age.
Teste., John B. Hilleary, James Q. Harvey, Stewart L. Queen.
Bk. A, p. 28.   /15/

COINER /COYNER/, CHRISTIAN, Upshur County, Va., 16 Nov., 1857; Dec. term, 1857.
Sons, ROBERT COINER, DAVID E. COINER, MICHAEL COINER, JOSEPH COINER, daus. JANE FAUGHT, ELIZABETH COINER, CATHERINE YONTS, MARGARET LEONARD, children of daus. MARY WOODS and NANCY MILLER, deceased, ANDREW RUSSELL, (relationship not shown). Son Robert Coyner, ex.
Testator desires pmt. of debts from sale of personalty; remainder of proceeds from sale to be divided equally among daus. JANE FAUGHT, ELIZABETH COINER, CATHERINE YONTS, children of testator's deceased daus., MARY WOODS, and NANCY MILLER; preceding bequest also to apply to any money due testator; to

(16, 17)

dau. MARGARET LEONARD and heirs, 10 a. "off north end of lot
number two of home farm"; to daus. JANE FAUGHT and ELIZABETH
COINER, and their heirs 42½ a. and house on home farm; to son
ROBERT COINER, 110 a. of home farm with provision that he give
to testator's son Joseph lot #3 of home farm being 105 a. and
to sd. Margaret Leonard her bequest of 10 a.; to son DAVID
COINER, 130 a. of home farm adjoining Ligget land on west; to
son MICHAEL "farm on east side of Buckhannon River where he resides probably 107 a"; also to son MICHAEL $200 to be pd. by
David and Joseph; remaining 5 a. of home tract to be sold at
public auction and proceeds divided equally among afsd. daus.
and grandchildren; sons Robert, Joseph, David, and Michael
each to pay daus. Jane Faught and Elizabeth Coiner $10 annual-
ly for support of ANDREW RUSSEL as long as he lives.
   Teste., J. B. McLean, George Bastable.
   Bk. A, pp. 29, 30.   /16/

   LAWHORN, LINDSEY, Upshur County, Va., 9 Nov., 1857; Dec.
term, 1857.
   Children MARTHA JANE, HESEKIAH, SARAH C., ELIZABETH,
ELIZA, JOSEPH A., and JAMES K. P.   K. Hopkins, ex.
   Testator desires pmt. of debts and funeral expenses from
sale of property; remainder of proceeds of sale to be held by
executor for use of infant children of testator viz., MARTHA
JANE, HESEKIAH, SARAH C., ELIZABETH, ELIZA E., JOSEPH A. and
JAMES K. P.
   Teste., Jacob Heavner, Gideon Heavner.
   Bk. A, pp. 27, 28.   /17/

   JACKSON, W/ILLIAM/ W., Upshur County, Va., 24 June 1858;
July term, 1858.
   Wife LUCY S. JACKSON, bros. JACOB J. JACKSON, GEORGE R.
JACKSON, sister REBECCA, JOHN M. A. JACKSON (relationship not
shown), WILLIAM TRASK (relationship not shown).   Bro. George
R. Jackson, ex.
   Testator desires pmt. of debts and funeral expenses from
funds provided; "bequeaths to wife LUCY S. JACKSON and her heirs
the house and lot on which I now reside with apurtenances in
fee simple bounded as follows: beginning at a stake standing
on a river bank between the river and the turnpike corner of
H. O. Middleton's land, running thence up said river with its
meanders towards the Mill to a stake on the river bank, thence
crossing S & P turnpike at right angles from the said stake so
as to pass house occupied by Thomas S. Russell on the west side
thereof about nine feet from said house, continuing said line
northwardly to the river and across said river to my line,
thence with said line up river to stake, mine and H. O. Middleton corner, thence with the line between mine and H. O. Middleton's land southwardly to the beginning.   Also to wife LUCY
three cows, three hogs, and all household and kitchen furniture
to dispose of as she sees fit, excepting one bed and thirty
yards of woolen carpet also to said LUCY one half of the clear
profits arising from my mills and machines from the time of my

death until same are sold by executor, also the growing crops
I now have in the ground. To JOHN M. A. JACKSON /does not
give relationship, but he was an adopted son/ one bed and bedding and thirty yards of woolen carpeting which Lucy S. Jackson
is to furnish him when he becomes of age or married /detailed
description of blankets, pillows, etc./. To JOHN M. A. JACKSON
and WILLIAM TRASK my real estate at mouth of Buckhannon River,
for which I hold four separate title bonds for four separate
pieces of land all adjoining. One of sixty and one half acres
purchased from E. N. Wells; one seventeen acres purchased from
Henry Criss; one five acres purchased from Abraham Reger also
mill site condemned thereon; executor to deliver title bonds
after my death to two men just mentioned; to same, turning
lathe and tools together with circular saws, etc., --- also
old carding machines and equipment in consideration of which
they be charged with amount of an execution levied thereon of
upwards of forty dollars in favor of Bastable and Haselden,
for use of Bastable, to the minister $11 who preaches my funer-
al sermon from money collected by executor after settling outstanding debts and selling real and personal estate not already
devised /mentions Sutton Mill property in Braxton County/.
Out of residue of proceeds two hundred dollars to be used in
mason work and tombstones to be placed at grave of my first
wife Charlotte Jackson and my own, marble slab to be placed
over each grave upon top of mason work with proper inscriptions.
Twenty-five from same fund to be applied as my wife Lucy may
direct for tombstones at grave of her daughter Mary Ella Parrack.
One hundred and fifty dollars of said sum to be used by executor George R. Jackson, my brother, for education of John M. A.
Jackson. If money is not expended before he attains twenty-
one years or marries said remaining sum shall be turned over
to him. After compensating my executor liberally the balance
remaining to be divided as follows: To LUCY S. JACKSON, Wife
one half (including house and lot valued at one thousand dollars)
other half equally divided between two brothers, JACOB J. and
GEORGE R. JACKSON, Sister REBECCA and JOHN M. A. JACKSON. If
any devisees obstruct the execution they shall forfeit their
rights etc. and their share shall go to wife Lucy S. Jackson."
       Teste., Henry F. Westfall, E. J. Colerider.
       Bk. A, pp. 31-34.   /18/

       LEWIS, JOHN, Upshur County, Va., 21 Nov. 1858; Dec. term,
1858.
       Wife not named, sons ISAAC LEWIS, JAMES LEWIS, JOHN LEWIS,
MARSHALL LEWIS, daus. ELIZABETH HESS, MALINDA HINKLE, and
LOUISA LEWIS, CEMANTHA, dau. of Adam LEWIS, deceased /relation-
ship not shown/. Son Isaac Lewis, ex.
       Testator desires pmt. of funeral expenses; bequeaths to
wife, not named, 1/3 of two homestead farms and ¼ of personalty during lifetime; to son ISAAC LEWIS, prior gifts and $1;
to son JAMES LEWIS, $450, a horse called "Pete" and 3 sheep;
to sons JOHN and MARSHALL LEWIS, equal division of two homestead farms; also to sd. JOHN, a gray horse, bridle, and saddle;

also to sd. MARSHALL a sorrel mare, bridle, and saddle; to dau.
ELIZABETH HESS and heirs, prior gifts and $350, Isaac Lewis to
act as her trustee; to dau. MALINDA HINKLE, prior gifts and
$300; to dau. LOUISA LEWIS, $300, saddle, cow, 3 sheep, bedding
"and bedclothes" when she leaves her mother; to CEMANTHA, rear-
ed by testator and dau. of Adam LEWIS, deceased, a bed, a cow,
and $100 "providing she remains with her aunt and is a good
girl until she is of age"; all realty and personalty not devised to be sold and proceeds distributed to provide for afsd.
bequests to "James and the girls", any deficit to be pd. by
sons John and Marshall or if surplus to be equally distributed
among all children.
    Teste., S. Rohrbough, Abram Post, Lare Deen.
    Bk. A, pp. 35-37.   /19/

    JACKSON, CARALINE, Upshur County, Va., 9 Dec. 1858; Dec.
term, 1858.
    Husband PETER JACKSON, dau. MARY LOUISA JACKSON.   Son
Robertson Jackson, ex.
    Testatrix desires pmt. of debts and funeral expenses; be-
queaths to hus. PETER JACKSON, use of homestead and maintenance from land with provision that he care for testator's dau.
MARY LOUISA, until she marries; at death of sd. Peter, land to
revert to testatrix's heirs.
    Teste., George D. White, John G. Dix.
    Bk. A, pp. 37, 38.   /20/

    VINCENT, JOHN, Upshur County, Va., 13 Jan. 1855; Feb.
term, 1859.
    Wife SARAH VINCENT, sons JOHN VINCENT, W. VINCENT, daus.
NANCY MEEK, NECY GOULD, SUSANNAH CHIDESTER, LUCY WILSON,
HEZEKIAH RIN (relationship not shown). No ex. named.
    Testator desires pmt. of debts and funeral expenses from
personalty; bequeaths to wife SARAH VINCENT, all realty and
personalty for life; upon death of sd. Sarah estate to testator's son JOHN VINCENT for life; after death of sd. John property to be equally divided among testator's children and their
heirs as follows: W. VINCENT, NANCY MEEK, NECY GOULD'S heirs,
SUSANNAH CHIDESTER, LUCY WILSON if she be a widow at time of
sd. John's death if not to receive only $10; if HEZEKIAH RIN
should survive sd. wife Sarah he is to be cared for by Susannah
Chidester out of the estate.
    Teste., Lewis Lundcefore /Lunceford/, David Bennett.
    Bk. A, pp. 40, 41.   /21/
    Codicil: 11 Mar. 1858.
    Provision allowing LUCY WILSON changed to equal division
of estate with provision that her husband John Wilson have no
management or control of bequest.
    Teste., David Bennett, Benjamin Gould.
    Renunciation: 11 Jan. 1860; 16 Jan. 1860 by SARAH VINCENT,
widow of JOHN VINCENT.

Renounces will of JOHN VINCENT and seeks to recover dower right and destributive share of realty and personalty as if sd. husband had died intestate.
Teste., James F. Cochran, Maranda H. Rexroad.
Bk. A, p. 42.

ROHRBOUGH, JOHN M., Upshur County, Va., 18 Apr. 1859; May term, 1859.
Wife MATILDA, sons CLARK L., WILLIAM H., son-in-law SETH WILLIAMS. Wife Matilda Rohrbough, ex.
Testator desires wife Matilda to sell ½ of threshing machine, wagon, young cattle and other personalty needed to pay debts and funeral expenses; to son WILLIAM H., 1 calf; to wife MATILDA residue of all realty and personalty until youngest son CLARK L. is of legal age when distribution to be made as follows: to wife MATILDA, 1/3 of property; remaining 2/3 to be equally divided among children /not named/ and consideration to be made of prior gifts, daus. who may have married to be given such assistance as sd. Matilda sees fit; to SETH WILLIAMS, husband of testator's dau. Elizabeth, property valued at $120 given them at time of marriage and $25 which sd. Williams owed testator.
Teste., A. M. Bastable, P. F. Pinnell.
Bk. A, pp. 38, 39.   /22/

HOOFMAN, JOSEPH /formerly of Hampshire County, Va./ Upshur County, Va., 18 Feb. 1856; Feb. term, 1861.
Sons ANDREW, JOHN, AMOS, JOSEPH, and ANTHONY, daus. SARAH SWISHER, ANNE MICHAEL, and ELIZA LANDAKER. Sons Amos and Anthony I. Hoofman, exs.
Testator desires to be "decently interred according to the rules and customs of the country"; bequeaths to son ANDREW, $100 "in good current money"; to son JOHN, $100; to son AMOS, $100; to son ANTHONY, $100; to dau. SARAH SWISHER, $50; to dau. ANNE MICHAEL, $25; to dau. ELIZA LANDAKER, $1, sd. daus. having received prior gifts; to son JOSEPH, residue of personalty and realty, also "large family Bible" with provision that testator make his home with sd. Joseph.
Teste., David Bosely, Henry Bean (his mark), John W. Bean (his mark).
Bk. A, pp. 43, 44.   /23/

TOLBERT, SAMUEL T., Upshur County, Va., 3 Jan. 1861; March and May terms, 1861.
Wife not named, sons DAVID J., GEORGE M., daus. MARGARET SMITH, ELIZABETH LANHAM, LYIA PETERSON, SARAH ARMSTRONG, grdson. SAMUEL T. LANHAM. Sons, David and George M. Tolbert, exs.
Testator bequeaths to son DAVID J. "part of home place bounded to wit: beginning at a hickory tree, a corner to other lands of said David and John Strader, and running thence eastwardly with the fence to the forks of the Ditch at the lower end of the medow, thence northwardly to a stake and poplar stump on the north side of the turnpike, corner to

lands of George M. Tolbert, thence westwardly with the turnpike ten poles. thence northwardly a straight line across the
field to a stake at the point of which George M. Tolbert's
meadow fence intersects mine and said George division fence,
thence with said George (the said division fence) to a line
of the other land of the said David thence with the said David's
line around to the beginning including the mansion house, orchard and appurtenances and containing about thirty eight acres,
for and in consideration of the said David J. shall pay to my
executors hereafter named the sum of twelve hundred and seventy
three dollars and thirty three and one half cents in three
equal, annual payments (one, two and three years) after my
death for the payments of my debts, but it is understood that
my wife is to retain a life estate in it and one third of said
land hereby devised "Dower right." To my son GEORGE M. TOLBERT
a certain portion of my home place, which portion so devised
to the said George is bounded as follows to wit, Beginning at
the aforesaid stake and poplar Stump on the north side of said
Turnpike and running westwardly across the field as aforesaid
to the division line fence between me and said George at the
point at which his meadow fence intersects it as aforesaid,
thence eastwardly and southwardly with said George lines to
the Beginning Stake and stump aforesaid, thence southwardly
with said Davids said Second line revised to the forks of the
Ditch, thence eastwardly with the fence to the road at the
North East Corner of an orchard, thence northwardly with the
road leading out to the turnpike until it strikes David Bennett
and my line, thence westwardly with said line and said George
line to the Beginning, with its appurtenances, containing
about 35 acres, for and in consideration whereof the said George
M. Tolbert shall pay to my said Executors seven hundred dollars
in one and two years after my death, for the payment of my
debts, but the said George is to take said land subject to my
wife's "Dower right". I give and devise to my Daughter MARGARET
SMITH the wife of Martin J. Smith a certain portion of my home
place Beginning on mine and David Bennett line on the road running southwardly from James Bennett's Tanyard, and running
thence Eastwardly with mine and Bennets lines to John Douglass
line, thence Southwardly with said Douglass, line of Jared
Armstrong's line thence with said Armstrong's lines to a line
of lands heretofore conveyed by me to said David J. Tolbert,
thence westwardly with said Davids line to the road aforesaid
thence with said road to the Beginning containing 20 acres,
and valued to her at $35 per acre and given to her to make
her even with my other children. To my daughter ELIZABETH
LANHAM one hundred and fifty acres of land to be selected by
her or her heirs out of any land which I own, excepting the
home place, But in laying off said 150 acres it is not to be
so laid off as to destroy the value of the residue of the
tract out of which it may be taken, but she or her heirs may
select any part of such tract that she or they may prefer, also to said Elizabeth the use of the residue of my home place
for the term of five years, commencing at the time of my death.

(24, 25)

To my wife one bedstead, bed and necessary bedding, my cupboard and its contents, one table (her choice) her life estate
in one third of the land aforesaid devised to my sons George
and David, in lieu of her dower right in and distribution share
of my real and personal estate. To my grand son SAMUEL T.
LANHAM one hundred acres of any of my unimproved (wild) lands
of average quality to be selected and located by my sons George
and David, I also give him one yearlin (iron gray) colt also,
two yearlin steers, but the said colt and cattle are to remain
under the control of my sons until the said Samuel T. Lanham
arrives at the age of 21 years, until which time he shall have
no disposing powers over the same. All the rest and residue
of my estate both real and personal I devise to my executors
hereinafter named to be sold by them upon such terms as they
may think best, and the proceeds thereof, together with the
proceeds of any bonds notes and accounts due to me shall be
equally divided between my six children GEORGE M. TOLBERT,
DAVID J. TOLBERT, ELIZABETH LANHAM, MARGARET SMITH, LYIA
PETERSON and SARAH ARMSTRONG. Should the $1273.33 and the
$700 which my sons David and George are required to pay as
aforesaid be more than is required to pay my debts and funeral
expenses, the balance remaining I desire to be equally divided
between them. But if not sufficient I desire the balance to be
paid out of the proceeds of·sale and distribution."
Teste., R. H. Townsend, G. W. Berlin.
Bk. A, pp. 47-50.   /24/

FULTZ, JOHN, Upshur County, Va., 31 May 1861; Aug. term,
1861.
Wife LEAH FULTZ, heir and ex.
Testator desires pmt. of debts and funeral expenses from
sale of personalty; ex. to sell at public auction all personalty other than that which she received from her father at time
of her marriage; sd. wife to have all household and kitchen
furniture; testator had an article of agreement with Jacob
Waugh dated Nov. 27, 1860 that $300 should be pd. by Nov. 1,
1862 of which $150 has been pd.; ex. to rent out land, leased
from sd. Waugh until such time as Waugh completes pmt. of $300
loaned to him; ex. to collect outstanding debts and invest in
land for benefit "of the expected heir to be born of testator's
wife in a proper time after death of testator"; if no heir sur-
vives land so purchased to wife LEAH for life then to be equally divided among testator's bros. and sisters (not named);
Lewis Carrykoff and Noey B. Wamsley to supervise purchase of
land.
Teste., N. B. Wamsley, Joseph W. Blosser.
Bk. A, pp. 44-46.   /25/

CLARK, CORNELIUS, Upshur County, Va., 23 July, 1861; Nov.
term, 1861.
Wife LUCINDA CLARK. No ex. named.
Testator bequeaths to wife LUCINDA CLARK all realty and

(26-28)

personalty for life to be disposed of at her death to children (not named) as she sees fit.
Teste., James L. Curry, Earl E. Zoung.
Bk. A, p. 47. /26/

REESE, SOLOMON, Upshur County, Va., 19 Nov. 1861; Jan. term, 1862.
Wife ELIZABETH, sons DAVID, JONATHAN, SAMUEL, daus. SARAH ROLLINS, ELIZABETH ROLLINS, JANE WESTFALL, and REBECCA REESE. No ex. named.
Testator bequeaths to wife ELIZABETH use of "mansion house" for life time, also 4 sheep, 1 cow, a small spinning wheel, 1 bed and bedding, 1/3 of crops; to son DAVID REESE, 20 a. and 24 poles of land "where he now resides" with provision that he pay to testator's son JONATHAN REESE, $35 in 2 years from date of will; to son SAMUEL REESE, 54 a. of land on which testator resides with provision that sd. Samuel pay $200 to each of testator's daus. SARAH ROLLINS, ELIZABETH ROLLINS, JANE WESTFALL, and REBECCA REESE, to be pd. in installments of $100 in 2 yrs. and equal pmt. at end of 4 yrs.; wife ELIZABETH and dau. REBECCA to have life use of mansion house; to son JONATHAN REESE, $35 to be pd. by sd. David; to dau. REBECCA, bed and bedding, large spinning wheel, loom "and its weaving contents"; to dau. SARAH ROLLINS, $50 to be pd. by son Samuel; to dau. ELIZABETH ROLLINS, $50 to be pd. by son Samuel; to dau. JANE WESTFALL, $50 to be pd. by son Samuel; residue of property to son SAMUEL with provision that he "pay off a bond I executed /to/ T. Janny for Thirty dollars or there about."
Teste., N. B. Wamsley, A. S. Rollins.
Bk. A, pp. 50, 51. /27/

COLERIDER, HENRY, Buckhannon, Upshur County, Va., 3 Jan. 1859; 20 Mar. 1862.
Wife ELEANOR, dau. MARY WILLIAMS. Wife Eleanor Colerider, ex.
Testator desires pmt. of debts and funeral expenses from personalty; bequeaths to wife ELEANOR all estate to use as she sees fit with exception of bequest to dau. MARY, wife of William H. WILLIAMS, $100.
Teste., Henry F. Westfall, N. G. Monday.
Bk. A, pp. 53, 54. /28/

CURRENCE, JOHN W., Upshur County, Va., 14 Feb. 1862; Mar. term, 1862.
Wife JOANNA, sons ADAM M. CURRENCE, SAMUEL M. CURRENCE, daus. MARGARET E. GIBSON, OCADEVIER TENNEY, CATHARINE E. BLACK, MARTHA JANE ZICKEFOOSE and SARAH MELISSA CURRENCE, dau-in-law REBECCA ANN CURRENCE. Wife Joanna Currence and Patrick Crickard, exs.
Testator desires pmt. of debts and funeral expenses from estate; bequeaths to wife JOANNA, 25 a. of land on which testator resides for life use, and at her death to son ADAM M. CUR-

(29-31)

RENCE, also "the improved portion of the residue of the Tyre
land not unsold," also gray horse, 2 cows, all kitchen and
household furniture; to son SAMUEL M. CURRENCE, 20 a. of the
Tyre land; to REBECCA ANN, wife of testator's son George W.
CURRENCE, 33 a. of land for "which she holds title bond"; to
son ADAM M. CURRENCE, 25 a. of the Tyre land "including the
four acre lot with house thereon which was purchased of Lyia
Tenney"; proceeds from sale of remainder of Tyre land to be
equally divided among testator's daus. MARGARET E. GIBSON,
OCADEVIER TENNEY, CATHARINE E. BLACK, MARTHA JANE ZICKEFOOSE,
and SARAH MELISSA CURRENCE; to wife, JOANNA all sheep, hogs and
farming equipment and at her death to son ADAM CURRENCE.
    Teste., N. B. Wamsley, P. Crickard.
    Bk. A, pp. 52, 53.   /29/

    BLACK, JAMES, (written by E. T. Summerville, friend) Bull
Run, Upshur County, Va., 6 Jan. 1862; 16 June 1862.
    Wife LEAN, sons CLARK M., CHAPMAN, and JAMES MARSHALL,
daus. LUCINDA and MANDA. Wife Lean Black, ex., friend E. T.
Summerville to act if she dies and to serve as her advisor.
    Testator desires pmt. of debts immediately; bequeaths to
wife LEAN all realty and personalty for life use; sd. Lean to
dispose of bay horse and sorrell mare and other property to
pay 3 installments yet due on home farm and to sell 14 a. of
land if needed; after death of wife to son CLARK, $5; to son
CHAPMAN, $5; to dau. MANDA, $5; to dau. LUCINDA, $5; to son
JAMES MARSHALL residue of estate.
    Teste., E. T. Summerville, A. W. C. Lemons, Isaac Lewis.
    Bk. A, pp. 54, 55.   /30/

    CLARK, JACOB, Upshur County, Va., 21 May 1862; 18 June
1862.
    Wife SUSANNA M., son WILLIAM M., and other children not
named. Anthony Reger, ex.
    Testator desires pmt. of debts and funeral expenses "out
of my money, twenty dollars" and other personalty; bequeaths
to wife SUSANNA M., remainder of personalty except horse,
saddle and bridle; to son WILLIAM M., sd. horse, saddle and
bridle and proceeds of the sale of 2 cows, 1 heifer and 8
yearling cattle, the latter bequest to pay taxes for present
yr. any remaining money to be placed on interest and divided
equally as "the children" arrive at the age of 18 with exception of sd. William M.; to sd. SUSANNA M., proceeds of land
"conveyed to me from Jacob Strader" for widowhood; when youngest child is of legal age ex. to sell all realty for 1/3 cash,
remainder to be pd. in one and two yr. installments and equal
division to be made among heirs, 1/3 to sd. SUSANNA if she is
still testator's widow, pmts. to be made to her annually.
    Teste., R. H. Clark, J. T. Regar, Peter Westfall.
    Bk. A, p. 56.   /31/

(32-34)

DIGHT, HENRY, Pvt. Co. D., 10th Va. Vol. Inf., detailed as Regimental Clerk, Upshur County, Va., 1 Sept. 1862; Oct. term, 1862.
    Mother, ELIZABETH HANNAH DIGHT. Simeon Rohrbough, ex.
    Testator desires pmt. of debts; bequeaths to mother ELIZABETH HANNAH DIGHT, all money due testator and any which may be in his possession at time of death.
    Teste., L. M. Marsh, Thomas C. Harrison, E. C. Marple, Anthony Rohrbough, E. Brake.
    Bk. A, p. 57.   /32/

MULLINS, JAMES, Upshur County, Va., 4 Apr. 1859; June term, 1863.
    Wife, MARY ANN, children not named. Mifflen Lorentz, ex.
    Testator desires pmt. of debts and funeral expenses to be pd. from receipts of sale of store house and stocks of goods and bills collected by ex.; bequeaths to wife MARY ANN, remaining proceeds from sd. sale, also dwelling house, two lots, household and kitchen furniture, with provision that should any of children leave home sd. Mary Ann is to give them "a bed or anything else she can spare"; in case of sd. Mary Ann's remarriage, property to be sold, she to receive 1/3, remainder to be equally divided among heirs; in case she does not remarry, property to be sold upon her death and divided equally among heirs.
    Teste., Joseph Flint, Nathan Reger.
    Bk. A, pp. 58, 59.   /33/

REEDER, AMOS, Upshur County, Va., 19 Feb. 1861; Upshur County, W. Va.; 9 Nov. 1863.
    Wife MAHALA REEDER, BROOMFIELD B. CURTES (relationship not shown). Wife Mahala Reeder, ex.
    Testator bequeaths to wife MAHALA REEDER all realty and personalty after pmt. of funeral expenses; upon death of sd. Mahala realty and personalty to BROOMFIELD B. CURTES "provided he has stayed with .... and taken care of Mahala during her life."
    Teste., Booth Bond, Joseph Flint.
    Bk. A, p. 60.   /34/

THOMPSON, ANDREW SR., Upshur County, Va., 9 Jan. 1861; Upshur County, W. Va., 14 Dec. 1863.
    Wife (not named), dau. CATHARINE, son ANDREW THOMPSON JR. Henry Simpson, ex.
    Testator desires pmt. of debts and funeral expenses; bequeaths to wife (not named) negro slaves Wesley, Matelda and Adeline for life use, also household and kitchen furniture, also $300 to be pd. by ex. in lieu of her dower right in other property; remainder of realty and personalty, in addition to afsd. slaves upon death of testator's widow to be divided equally in two parts; to dau. CATHARINE, one share of afsd. estate; to Levi Leonard, trustee, remaining share of estate to be held in trust for testator's son ANDREW THOMPSON JR., for

(35-38)

his natural life, "free from his debts and liabilities present
and future" with provision that trustee pay to sd. Andrew Jr.,
annually, all rents, interest, and profits to be used for his
maintenance, sd. Andrew Jr. to support and care for his mother;
trustee to have privilege of selling any property he may desire
and sd. Andrew Jr. to have use of any property; upon death of
sd. Andrew Jr., property to be equally divided among his heirs.
    Teste., G. W. Berlin, A. Poundstone.
    Bk. A, pp. 61, 62.   /35/

    CUTRIGHT, MATILDIA, Upshur County, Va., 31 Dec. 1862;
Upshur County, W. Va., 14 Mar. 1864.
    Sisters ISIBLE CUTRIGHT, PERMELIA CUTRIGHT, CATHARINE
CUTRIGHT. No ex. named.
    Testatrix bequeaths to sisters ISIBLE CUTRIGHT, PERMELIA
CUTRIGHT, and CATHARINE CUTRIGHT, equal division of all realty
and personalty.
    Teste., George Clark, Abram Strader.
    Bk. A, p. 63.   /36/

    CUTRIGHT, CATHARINE, Upshur County, W. Va., 21 Oct. 1863;
14 Mar. 1864.
    Sisters ISIBLE CUTRIGHT and PERMELIA CUTRIGHT. No ex.
named.
    Testatrix bequeaths to sisters ISIBLE and PERMELIA CUT-
RIGHT equal division of all realty and personalty.
    Teste., George Clark, Asby P. Cutright.
    Bk. A, pp. 63, 64.   /37/

    CUTRIGHT, ISIBLE, Upshur County, W. Va., 28 Feb. 1864;
14 Mar. 1864.
    Sister PERMELIA CUTRIGHT. No ex. named.
    Testatrix bequeaths to sister PERMELIA CUTRIGHT all realty
and personalty.
    Teste., George Clark, Asahel Cutright.
    Bk. A, p. 64.   /38/

    LIGGETT, JOSEPH, Upshur County, Va., 12 Apr. 1861; Upshur
County, W. Va., 11 Apr. 1864.
    Wife ELIZABETH, sons LEVI, NATHAN, AARON, and ALVIN M.,
daus. MARY MILLS, ELIZABETH ANN CLARK, JANE LIGGETT, SUSAN
LIGGETT, REBECCA ANN LIGGETT, BARBARA LIGGETT. Ex. not named.
    Testator desires pmt. of debts, sd. pmt. to be made by
son Alvin M. Liggett; bequeaths to elder sons LEVI, NATHAN, and
AARON prior gift of land "known Devine place and lands bought
of John Hoy, lying on waters of Glady Fork of Stone Coal"; to
son ALVIN M., remainder of realty and personalty with provision that he care for testator's widow ELIZABETH LIGGETT during
her lifetime and pay following bequests; to testator's daus.
MARY MILLS, ELIZABETH ANN CLARK, JANE LIGGETT, SUSAN LIGGETT,
REBECCA ANN LIGGETT, and BARBARA LIGGETT, $400 each, first
pmt. of sd. bequest to be pd. to Elizabeth Ann Clark and Mary
Mills 6 mos. after death of sd. Elizabeth Liggett and semi-

(39-41)

annually thereafter until complete; pmt. to sd. Jane, Susan, Rebecca Ann and Barbara to begin one yr. after completion of preceding bequest.
 Teste., D. L. Haselden, Orr Lawson.
 Bk. A, p. 65.   /39/

 GOULD, AARON, Upshur County, Va., 29 Feb. 1856; Upshur County, W. Va., 14 June 1864.
 Wife CALYSTA GOULD, sons SAMUEL and DANIEL. No. ex. named.
 Testator desires pmt. of debts and funeral expenses; bequeaths to son SAMUEL GOULD any notes or bonds given by sd. Samuel to testator in pmt. for land where sd. Samuel now resides; to wife CALYSTA all personalty and realty, with exception of land now occupied by son DANIEL GOULD; at death of wife Calysta realty to be equally divided among all heirs with exception of son Daniel "who has received his equal part in land sold him at much less than value."
 Teste., David Bennett, Abigal Bennett, Virginia Bennett.
 Bk. A, p. 66.   /40/

 TENNEY, LYDIA, Upshur County, W. Va., 7 Mar. 1864; 1 July 1864.
 Dau. DORCAS HANEY, son JOSIAH TENNEY, grdau. ELIZABETH HANEY, other heirs (relationship not shown) ELIZABETH, wife of Daniel PHIPPS, ELIZA J., wife of G. F. KITTLE, JOSIAH TENNEY, CERENEANN, wife of Addison TENNEY, and heirs of John L. Tenney, deceased. Watson Westfall, friend, ex.
 Testatrix desires pmt. from personalty of debts, funeral expenses and purchase of "tombstones small and cheap for graves of Josiah Tenney, my deceased husband and for testatrix, and to enclose in palens (sic) enough ground to bury all the children of Josiah by the side of him if they desire to be buried in the same graveyard"; to dau. DORCAS HANEY, a grey mare with provision that she raise a colt for sd. Dorcas' dau. ELIZABETH HANEY; also to DORCAS HANEY, mansion house and all land deeded to testator by heirs of Josiah Tenney, deceased; also to sd. DORCAS HANEY "a small portion on the west side of the public road leading up Truby's Run and is to embrace the land from the road adjoining Peter Tenney up to said Tenney corner, thence to run an eastward direction to a Oak bush by the road some two or three poles from the sulphur springs"; to son JOSIAH TENNEY or his heirs $10 to be collected from personalty by ex., sd. amount being due Josiah from his father; remainder of estate after pmt. of debts and funeral expenses to be equally divided among heirs of Josiah Tenney, deceased, namely ELIZABETH, wife of Daniel PHIPPS, ELIZA J., wife of G. T. KITTLE, JOSIAH TENNEY, CERENEANN, wife of Addison M. TENNEY, and heirs of JOHN L. TENNEY, deceased; pmt. to be made annually.
 Teste., Jaspor N. Westfall, Howard Rowan (his mark), Watson Westfall.
 Bk. A, pp. 67-69.   /41/

(42, 43)

STOUT, BENJAMIN, Upshur County, Va., 6 June 1863; Upshur County, W. Va., 11 Oct. 1864.
Wife MARTHA, dau. DEBORAH, sons GEORGE, HEZEKIAH, JOHN, DANIEL, and BENJAMIN. No ex. named.
Testator desires pmt. of debts; bequeaths to sons GEORGE and HEZEKIAH, equal division of all personalty and realty after pmt. of debts; should sd. sons George and Hezekiah "not return or die before my decease" estate to be equally divided among other sons; to dau. DEBORAH, $500 "provided no suit be entered by my wife Martha for a separate maintenance"; should such suit be entered then legacy to sd. Deborah is void and legacy to be divided among testator's sons GEORGE, HEZEKIAH, JOHN, DANIEL, and BENJAMIN, each to pay to sd. Deborah $100 when she arrives at age of 21, if no suit be brought.
Teste., John Bassel, Presby B. Beach.
Bk. A, p. 69.   /42/

JOHNS, ROBERT, Upshur County, Va. (sic), 30 May 1864; 13 Feb. 1865.
Wife PALSY, dau. MARTHA, sons DOUGLAS, ROBERT, and DAVIS K., grandson, ROBERT JOHNS. No ex. named.
Testator desires pmt. of debts and funeral expenses; also pmt. of note given by testator to John Brannon for land to be pd. equally by testator's sons; bequeaths to son DOUGLAS JOHNS, "provided he lives and gets home to occupy it," a lot of land "beginning on the old salt work road between J. W. Wilson and house of testator where the Newton line crosses the road thence with the same, crossing the Fall run and up a left hand branch to the first drain on the south side west of the lick and up the drain southward to the top of the ridge, to include a spring in said drain, towards the west fork to a birch and white oak, corner of land bought of Samuel Wilson to include all the land east of said line bought of said Wilson and Newton heirs"; if sd. Douglas does not return preceding legacy to son ROBERT JOHNS, also land bequeathed to son Davis K. Johns, if he does not return, Robert to pay heirs of Douglas and Davis K., $10 each, also to ROBERT, remaining land after deduction of bequests and dower right of testator's widow, also 1 horse after death of sd. widow; to son DAVIS K. JOHNS, "provided he get home to occupy it" a tract of land "beginning at the old salt work road where my line crosses the road west of the D. K. Johns house and with the road to testator's meadow fence so as to include a part of a good spring on Sugar Camp hollow, thence to the line of the land purchased of the Newton heirs and with the same to where Douglas Johns line will cross thence with the same South to a beech and W. O. Corner"; to grandson ROBERT JOHNS, one white mare and colt; to dau. MARTHA JOHNS, 4 sheep and 2 milch cows; to wife PALSY, remainder of personalty and dower right in realty bequeathed to sd. Robert and upon her death realty to son ROBERT.
Teste., David Bennett, James F. Friel.
Bk. A, pp. 70, 71.   /43/

(44-46)

DONNELLEY, JAMES, Upshur County, W. Va., 16 Jan. 1865;
8 May 1865.
Son JAMES N., daus. ELIZABETH A. WILLIAMS and MARGARET
McDOWELL. No ex. named.
Testator desires pmt. of debts and funeral expenses; be-
queaths to son JAMES N. DONNELLEY and heirs all realty and
personalty; to dau. ELIZABETH A. WILLIAMS, $1; to dau. MAR-
GARET McDOWELL, 1 feather bed.
Teste., James McAvoy, L. Y. McAvoy.
Bk. A, p. 72.   /44/

GEYER, BAZALELL, Upshur County, W. Va., 27 Oct. 1865;
15 Nov. 1865.
Wife MARTHA LEWIS ANN, mother MARY GEYER, bros. MICHAEL,
ABRAHAM M., HARVEY, and HENRY.   Bros., Michael and Harvey
Geyer, exs.
Testator bequeaths to bros. MICHAEL and ABRAHAM M. GEYER,
150 a. farm on which testator resides, with provision that be-
fore they take possession they pay to testator's wife MARTHA
LEWIS ANN GEYER, $500, also to maintain testator's mother
MARY GEYER during her lifetime, also to pay debts and funeral
expenses; to wife MARTHA LEWIS ANN, in addition to sd. bequest,
all livestock, household and kitchen furniture "and all crops
now grown on land"; to bros. MICHAEL, HARVEY, HENRY, and
ABRAHAM M., equal division of land inherited by testator from
his father.
Teste., Austin Griffin, R. H. Townsend.
Bk. A, pp. 74, 75.   /45/

WHITE, ISAAC, Montgomery County, Va., 30 Sept. 1865;
6 Nov. 1865; recorded Upshur County, W. Va., 22 Nov. 1865.
Wife MARY W. WHITE. Son A. C. White, ex.
Testator desires pmt. of debts from estate; bequeaths to
wife MARY W. WHITE, remaining personalty and realty located in
Upshur County, W. Va., "and elsewhere."
Teste:, Isaac White Jr., Mifflin Lorentz.
Bk. A, pp. 73, 74.   /46/

MORGAN, THEODORE, Upshur County, W. Va., 12 Nov. 1865;
14 Feb. 1866.
Wife LYDIA H., daus. MARIA L., LUCEBA, HARRIET, and GRACE
HANNAH, other heirs: MAXWELL W. MORGAN, heirs of A. B. MORGAN,
widow of M. B. MORGAN. Henry Jones, ex.
Testator desires pmt. of debts and funeral expenses from
personalty; all realty on French Creek to be sold at $30 per a.
within 1 yr. after testator's death; bequeaths to wife LYDIA
H. MORGAN, 1/3 of proceeds of sd. sale; to daus. MARIA L.,
LUCEBA, HARRIET, and GRACE HANNAH MORGAN, equal division of
remaining proceeds of sale; to wife LYDIA and afsd. daus.,
60 a. of land in Illinois; family to retain for their use the
wagon, buggy, hill side plow, shovel plow, 3 horses, $300;
remainder of personalty to be sold at public auction within

(47-49)

one yr. after testator's death and proceeds to be equally
divided among MAXWELL W. MORGAN, heirs of A. B. MORGAN, MARIA
L. MORGAN, LUCEBA MORGAN, HARRIET MORGAN, and GRACE MORGAN;
to widow of M. B. MORGAN, $100.
    Teste., A. P. Rusmisell, Daniel Gould.
    Bk. A, pp. 76, 77.   /47/

    B/E/ZLE, WILLIAM, Upshur County, Va., 8 Oct. 1861; Upshur
County, W. Va., 15 May 1866.
    Wife HANNAH, dau. HANNAH, HENRY BOFFMAN (relationship not
shown). No ex. named.
    Testator bequeaths to HENRY BOFFMAN, 27 a. of land being
home of testator and all personalty with provision that he
care for testator and wife HANNAH "providing them with food
and rainment during their lives and seeing that they are decently buried"; also that sd. Henry Boffman care for testator's dau.
HANNAH and "keep her in his home as long as she conducts herself in a becoming manner."
    Teste., Joseph Flint, Steven Norman.
    Bk. A, pp. 77, 78.   /48/

    IRELAND, ALEXANDER R., Warren Twsp., Upshur County, W. Va.,
27 Aug. 1865; 15 May 1866.
    Son JOHN, dau. MARY JANE /FARNSWORTH/, grandchildren
LAFAEETE L. LORENTZ, ALEXANDER M. LORENTZ, PERRY L. LORENTZ,
MARIETTA LORENTZ, and SARAH R. LORENTZ. Son John Ireland and
/son-in-law/ D. D. T. Farnsworth, exs.
    Testator bequeaths to grandchildren LAFAYETTE L., ALEXANDER
M., PERRY L., MARIETTA, and SARAH R. LORENTZ, $1,000 each from
personalty, if personalty not sufficient for pmt. of bequests
then testator's son John and dau. Mary Jane to complete pmt.
equally provided suit between testator and John Walden which was
pending at time will was made is settled in favor of testator;
if Walden wins sd. suit the afsd. legatees are to lose from legacy equal shares of costs and expenses connected with sd. suit,
together with equal share of value of land so lost "and payment
shall be withheld from them"; afsd. legacies to be pd. when sd.
heirs reach age of 21; also to same grandchildren proceeds of
sale of lots and houses in Buckhannon to be applied as pmt. of
sd. legacies; to testator's son JOHN IRELAND, 232 a. of land
"from the upper end of the tract of land of home place including the David Jackson tract a part of which is in dispute in
suit with John Walden"; if sd. suit is lost by testator, other
heirs to provide for preceding bequest; also to sd. JOHN IRELAND,
prior gift of $350; to dau. MARY JANE /FARNSWORTH/ and heirs,
$860, a prior gift from testator to D. T. Farnsworth /hus-
band of sd. Mary Jane/, also to sd. MARY JANE sufficient land
valued at $25 per acre to make her share equal to that of John
Ireland; to son JOHN and dau. MARY JANE, equal division of all
remaining realty, also equal division of all personalty after
pmt. of bequests, debts, and funeral expenses.
    Teste., John N. Loudin, O. B. Loudin.
    Bk. A, pp. 75-80.   /49/

(50-52)

LORENTZ, JACOB, Upshur County, W. Va., 21 June 1865; 16 May 1866.
Sons GEORGE W., JOHN, MARSHALL, PERRY, JACOB JR., MIFFLIN, JASPER N., VALENTINE J., dau. RUHANNAH POUNDSTONE, heirs of deceased daus. HARRIET KEE, POLLY REGER, and KATHERYN ROHR-BOUGH. Sons John and Mifflin Lorentz, exs.
Testator desires pmt. of debts and funeral expenses from sale of realty and personalty; bequeaths to son GEORGE W. LORENTZ, his wife and children, prior gifts amounting to not less than $11,648 in realty and personalty; to son JOHN LORENTZ, prior gifts amounting to $5,852.79; to son MARSHALL LORENTZ, prior gifts amounting to $9,156.60; to son PERRY LORENTZ, wife and children, prior gifts amounting to $8,482.46; to son JACOB LORENTZ JR., prior gifts amounting to $6,106.99; to son MIFFLIN LORENTZ, prior gifts amounting to $5,503; to son JASPER N. LORENTZ, wife, and children, prior gifts amounting to $5,753.84; to son VALENTINE LORENTZ, prior gifts amounting to $6,805.63; to heirs of testator's deceased dau. POLLY, wife of Nathan REGER, prior gifts amounting to $1,861.68; to heirs of testator's deceased dau. KATHERYN, wife of Simeon ROHRBOUGH, prior gifts amounting to $4,721.83; to heirs of testator's deceased dau. HARRIET, wife of John KEE, prior gifts amounting to $5,319.48; to dau. RUHANNAH, wife of Andrew POUNDSTONE, prior gifts amounting to $1,725.92; remainder of estate to be divided among afsd. heirs so that shares may be equalized.
Teste., George Allman, Paris Casto.
Bk. A, pp. 80-83.   /50/

OURS, JACOB, Upshur County, W. Va., 12 May 1866; 12 June 1866.
Wife MALINDA, dau. E. JANE OURS. Wife Malinda Ours, ex.
Testator bequeaths to wife MALINDA all personalty and realty for life use with exception of one tract on Buckhannon Fork of Hackers Creek, sd. tract to be sold and proceeds used for pmt. of debts; to dau. by former marriage E. JANE OURS, any remainder of proceeds from sd. sale; to sd. E. JANE OURS, $200 to be pd. one yr. after testator's death, funds for sd. pmt. to be raised from proceeds of afsd. sale or the sale of personalty sufficient to meet bequest.
Teste., J. N. Loudin, Layfaett E. DeBarr.
Bk. A, p. 86.   /51/

HURST, JOHN, Upshur County, W. Va., 12 Mar. 1867; 15 May 1867.
Wife MARY G., dau. LUCY, son CHARLES. Wife Mary G. Hurst, ex.
Testator bequeaths to wife MARY G. HURST all personalty, also house and lot "lying at the West end of Buckhannon town fronting on the Staunton and Parkersburg pike" for life; at death of sd. Mary property to be equally divided among children; house and lot on Locust St., to be sold soon after testator's death, proceeds from sale to sd. MARY G., for support of herself, dau. LUCY, and son CHARLES and for repairs to dwelling.
Teste., Jackman Cooper, Joseph Ward.
Bk. A, p. 87.   /52/

(53)

JOHNS, HARVEY, Upshur County, W. Va., 14 June 1867; 12
Aug. 1867.
Wife MARY E., daus. MARY ANN JOHNS, REBECCA SUSAN JOHNS,
other children not named. Son James Johns, ex.
Testator desires pmt. of debts and funeral expenses;
bequeaths to wife MARY E. JOHNS, a bond "due on Andrew Beverage
of Highland County," also "all the property she brought into
the family or its value in money and one sachel"; to dau. MARY
ANN JOHNS, $100 "when last bond on Thomas Rexroad is collected,"
also bedding "known as her own"; to dau. REBECCA SUSAN JOHNS,
$50, pmt. to be made at time mentioned in afsd. bequest; re-
mainder of estate to be equally divided "between all the children"; home farm to be rented until advantageous sale can be
made; bequests to minor children to be placed on interest until
they reach 21 yrs. of age; all property with exception of bedding to be sold as soon as possible after testator's death;
bedding to be divided equally among all children; Wm. N.
Childress and Wm. B. Hull to make sd. division.
Teste:, Wm. N. Childress, Peter Gumm, Lewis W. Ferrell.
Bk. A, pp. 88, 89.   /53/

MIDDLETON, HENRY O., Upshur County, W. Va., 21 Jan. 1867;
16 Oct. 1867.
Daus. JULIA A. MIDDLETON, ANNE E. BROWN, and ELLEN M.
DICKINSON, sons HENRY C. MIDDLETON and JAMES E. MIDDLETON,
grandson, CHARLES BROWN. Julia A. Middleton and James E.
Middleton, exs.
Testator bequeaths to dau. JULIA A. MIDDLETON, a moiety
of farm known as "Greenberry Point" in Ann Arundel County, Md.,
also a moiety of "all personalty thereon with house and kitchen
furniture," also $3,000 from sale of land or bonds subject to
trust to sd. Julia, or other trustees as Anne E. Brown may
prefer; to dau. ANNE E. BROWN, one moiety in "Greenberry Point,"
and personalty thereon to be held in trust by sd. Julia A.
Middleton for the use of sd. Anne E. Brown or her children,
also her equal share of the profits from the farm, sd. Julia
A. Middleton to have full possession and control as trustee;
to dau. ELLEN M. DICKINSON, $5,000 to be held in trust by her
husband James E. Dickinson for the use of sd. Ellen and her
children, sd. bequest to be pd. by exs. from sale of lands or
bonds; to son HENRY C. MIDDLETON, $1,000 in addition to prior
gifts of more than $20,000; to son JAMES E. MIDDLETON, $5,000
in addition to prior gifts; to grandson CHARLES BROWN, testator's gold watch; after pmt. of debts and legacies remainder
of estate to be distributed equally among sd. Ellen M. Dickinson,
Anne E. Brown, Julia A., Henry C., and James E. Middleton; exs.
to be allowed 10% commission to care for costs of administration.
Not witnessed. Each p. signed by testator.
Attachment, n.d.:
Testator had meant in clause one that dau. Julia A.
Middleton act as trustee for Anne E. Brown but gives sd. Anne
privilege of naming one of her own children if she so desires;
trustee to have no authority to dispose of any property with-

out written consent of sd. Anne E. Brown; trustees to keep
account of all funds; land not to be divided without consent
of all heirs; executors to qualify without bond.
Not witnessed.
Bk. A, pp. 89-92.   /54/

ROHRBOUGH, SIMON, Upshur County, W. Va., 2 Dec. 1867; 10
Dec. 1867.
Daus. HARRIET R., ELSE G., son, SIMON ELLIOTT ROHRBOUGH,
other children not named.   Sons Asbury B. and George M.
Rohrbough, exs.
Testator desires pmt. of debts and funeral expenses from
sale of personalty and realty; remainder of proceeds of sd.
sale to be equally divided among children (not named) with pro-
vision that prior gifts be considered in settlement; in addi-
tion to sd. bequests, $100 additional to each of daus. HARRIET
R. and ELSE G., and to son SIMON ELLIOTT.
Teste., John Smith, V. J. Lorentz.
Bk. A, p. 92.   /55/

OSBORN, WILSON, Upshur County, W. Va., 13 Apr. 1866; 10
Dec. 1867.
Wife SUSANNAH, sons MARCELLUS, EDWARD W., ALVIN, AQUILLA,
ELMORE, dau. AMANDA, children of dau. JULIA ANN.   Ex. not
named.
Testator desires pmt. of debts and funeral expenses; bequeaths to wife SUSANNAH, life use of all personalty and all
realty in Upshur County except "a certain boundary thereof"
which is bequeathed to son MARCELLUS; at death of sd. Susannah,
realty to youngest son EDWARD, should he remain at home; after
death of sd. Susannah, personalty to be equally divided among
children ALVIN, AQUILLA, ELMORE, MARCELLUS, and AMANDA; to
children of testator's dau. JULIA ANN, $5 to be equally divided
among them; to son MARCELLUS, a tract of land adjoining
Jeremiah Lanham with exception of timber thereon, sd. Marcellus
to pay estate for land at rate of $2.50 per acre, the price to
be deducted from sd. Marcellus' share of personalty.
Teste., William B. Lynch, Abram A. Smith.
Bk. A, pp. 93, 94.   /56/

LANDES, DANIEL, Upshur County, W. Va., 12 Sept. 1867; 13
Jan. 1868.
Son JAMES WILLIAM FRANKLIN LANDES, dau. not named, step-
dau. LOUISA S. YEATES. Son James W. F. Landes, ex.
Testator bequeaths to son JAMES WILLIAM FRANKLIN LANDES,
farm valued at $1,200, also ½ of present crops, also all stock
except one horse and one cow, also all farm equipment, also all
"saw timber appraised to him at valuation," also one half of
remaining personalty after pmt. of debts and funeral expenses;
to dau. (not named), one cow, also all household and kitchen
furniture, also ½ of remainder of personalty, also $600 to be
pd. by sd. James W. F. Landes to be pd. in annual pmts. of $100,

first pmt. to be made 4 yrs. after testator's death; to step-
dau. LOUISA S. YEATES, $100 to be pd. equally by sd. son and
dau. within 10 yrs. after testator's death, sd. Louisa S.
Yeates to make her home with sd. James W. F. Landes until she
marries.
    Teste., William H. Davis, Mansfield Marshall, John Ruff,
and David Landes.
    Bk. A, pp. 95, 96.   /57/

    GEYER, ABRAM M., Upshur County, W. Va., 26 Oct. 1867;
7 Feb. 1868.
    .   Bros. WILLIAM F., HENRY, HARVEY and MICHAEL GEYER. Harvey
Geyer, ex.
    Testator desires pmt. of debts and funeral expenses from
collection of 2 notes, one for $92.66 2/3 and one for $70 due
from George S. Riffle; bequeaths to bro. WILLIAM F. GEYER,
his note for $90; to bro. HARVEY GEYER, $30 from collection of
sd. notes; to bro. MICHAEL GEYER, remainder of collection of
sd. notes; to bros. Michael and Harvey Geyer, equal division
of testator's bequest of land by will of his late father,
Michael Geyer.
    Teste., R. H. Townsend, C. S. Haynes.
    Bk. A, p. 96.   /58/

    KESLING, JOHN, Upshur County, W. Va., 22 Nov. 1867; 9
Mar. 1868.
    Wife ELIZABETH, daus. OLIVE HINKLE, JUDITH REGER, grand-
son JOHN WILLIAM WARNER, son-in-law GOODMAN REGER, son, NOAH N.
KESLING. Martin Hinkle, Goodman Reger or Noah N. Kesling, exs.
    Testator desires pmt. of debts and funeral expenses from
personalty; bequeaths to wife ELIZABETH, one mare, 2 cows, 6
sheep, all household and kitchen furniture, saddle and bridle
and $100, sd. property to remain hers if she remains a widow;
to dau. OLIVE, wife of Martin HINKLE, testator's silver watch
and a $200 bond held by testator on sd. Martin Hinkle, sd.
silver watch to be given upon death of sd. Olive to testator's
grandson JOHN WILLIAM WARNER, if sd. Olive die without issue
Martin Hinkle bond to testator's other heirs; to son-in-law
GOODMAN REGER, note for $150; to son NOAH N. KESLING, testa-
tor's home farm, farm equipment, and "rifle gun" with provision that he care for testator and testator's wife Elizabeth
during their lives; to grandson, JOHN WILLIAM WARNER, in addition to prior bequest, $200 to be pd. in pmts. of $100 when he
reaches age of 21 and 23 yrs.; to daus. OLIVE HINKLE and JUDITH
REGER, and to sd. John William Warner, equal division of proceeds arising from the collection of outstanding claims, notes,
and uncollected claims against the estate of Henry O. Middleton,
also all personalty not otherwise devised.
    Teste., G. Rogers, N. B. Wamsley.
    Bk. A, pp. 97, 98.   /59/

(60-63)

DESPER, THOMAS P., Upshur County, W. Va., 20 Aug. 1867;
9 June 1868.
Wife ROBERTA JANE, niece ELIZA JANE CUNNINGHAM, bro.
SHELTON DESPER. No ex. named.
Testator desires pmt. of debts and funeral expenses from
personalty; bequeaths to niece ELIZA JANE CUNNINGHAM, one bed
and bedding, one cow, 6 sheep, and $25 to be pd. when she
reaches 18 or marries, with provision that she remain with testator's wife until that time; to wife ROBERTA JANE, remainder
of personalty and all realty if she remains a widow, if she
remarries she may sell 100 a. of farm to be considered as her
dower; if widow remarries residue of estate to bro. SHELTON
DESPER.
Teste., E. E. Curry, James W. Windle, and D. Bennett.
Bk. A, p. 99.   /60/

BILBEE, MARY, Upshur County, W. Va., 25 Apr. 1868; 10 Aug.
1868.
Son HENRY BILBEE. Francis M. Rexroad, ex.
Testatrix desires pmt. of debts and funeral expenses; be-
queaths to son HENRY BILBEE and his heirs, all realty and per-
sonalty.
Teste., F. M. Rexroad, D. D. Linger, D. Bennett.
Bk. A, p. 100.   /61/

JOHNS, REBECCA, Upshur County, W. Va., 28 July 1868; 12
Oct. 1868.
Step-mother MARY E. JOHNS, bros. JAMES and WALTER JOHNS,
sisters MARY ANN and ELIZABETH JOHNS. Mary E. Johns, ex.
Testatrix desires pmt. of debts and funeral expenses; be-
queaths to bro. JAMES JOHNS, $1; to bro. WALTER JOHNS, $1; to
sister MARY ANN JOHNS, $1; to sister ELIZABETH JOHNS, $1; to
step-mother, MARY E. JOHNS, all household furniture and residue
of estate.
Teste., William N. Childress, A. S. Beverage, and J. S.
Beverage.
Bk. A, p. 101.   /62/

BODKINS, PATRICK, Upshur County, W. Va., 31 Oct. 1868;
14 Dec. 1868.
Sons PATRICK, JOHN, MARTIN, and PETER BODKINS, daus.
BRIDGET CONNELLY and MARY FINIGAN, son-in-law PATRICK FINIGAN.
Patrick Finigan, ex.
Testator desires pmt. of debts and funeral expenses from
personalty; bequeaths to son PATRICK BODKINS, prior gift of
one heifer; to son JOHN BODKINS, prior gift of $1; to son
MARTIN BODKINS, prior gift of $1; to son PETER BODKINS, prior
gift of one heifer; to dau. BRIDGET, now widow CONNELLY, prior
gift of $20; to dau. MARY FINIGAN and son-in-law PATRICK
FINIGAN, remainder of personalty.
Teste., Valentine Hinkle Jr., Johanney Conners.
Bk. A, p. 102.   /63/

(64, 65)

CRITES, LEONARD, Washington Tshp., Upshur County, W. Va.,
25 July 1866; 14 June 1869.
   Wife ELIZABETH, sons JACOB L., ABRAM C., JOHN D., WILLIAM
M., other heirs (relationship not shown) JOSEPH CRITES, ABRAM
CRITES, MARY CRITES, CATHERINE CRITES, REBECCA CRITES, LUCINDA
ESKEW, MAHALA DEAN, heirs of ELIZABETH LINGER. No ex. named.
   Testator bequeaths to son JACOB L. CRITES, 100 a. of land
on right hand fork of Buckhannon River including his residence;
to son ABRAM C. CRITES, mill and 15 a. of land "including the
channel of Buckhannon River from the mouth of Ben's Run to
the mill dam, and lying on the west bank of sd. river"; to
sons JOHN D. and WILLIAM M. CRITES, equal division of all improved and unimproved land east of the Buckhannon River; to
JOSEPH CRITES, ABRAM CRITES, MARY CRITES, CATHERINE CRITES and
REBECCA CRITES, equal division of unsold land west of Buckhannon River; to wife ELIZABETH CRITES, home farm and proceeds
therefrom, all household furniture "including stove"; sd. Mary,
Catherine, and Rebecca Crites to live at home and receive support from farm until they marry; to LUCINDA ESKEW, $250; to
MAHALA DEAN, one cow; to heirs of ELIZABETH LINGER, $130 each
when they reach age of 21; pmt. to be made equally by John D.
and William M. Crites.
   Teste., David C. Napier, Hanson R. Crites.
   Bk. A, pp. 103, 104.   /64/

   ROLLINS, PERMELIA, Meade Tshp., Upshur County, W. Va.,
11 June 1869; 12 July 1869.
   Husband EDMUND D. ROLLINS. No ex. named.
   Testatrix desires pmt. of funeral expenses from estate;
bequeaths to husband EDMUND D. ROLLINS "the home farm lying on
the west side of the Buckhannon River adjoining lands of Abram
Strader, Albert Cutright," sd. farm having been devised to
testatrix by wills of father William Cutright and sisters
Matilda, Isabella, and Catharine Cutright, also all personalty.
   Teste., Asby P. Cutright, Granvill S. Cutright, N. B.
Wamsley.
   Bk. A, p. 105.   /65/

   BARB, MOSES, Upshur County, W. Va., 9 June 1869; 13 Sept.
1869.
   Wife NANCY E., daus. MANERVY ANN McCLAIN, VIRGINIA MILLS,
MARY JANE CATHERINE /MILLS7, TURSEY GOODWIN, son PETER B.
BARB, step-sons PETER and JAMES BARB, GEORGE W. TENNEY (rela-
tionship not shown). No ex. named.
   Testator bequeaths to wife NANCY E. BARB, all household
and kitchen furniture, all live stock and home tract of land;
upon death of sd. Nancy E. Barb personalty to be divided equal-
ly among daus. MANERVY ANN, wife of William McCLAIN, VIRGINIA
MILLS and MARY JANE CATHERINE /MILLS7; realty to step-sons
PETER and JAMES BARB; to son PETER B. BARB, ½ of cabinet tools
and farm equipment and "rifle gun"; to step-sons PETER and
JAMES BARB, remainder of cabinet and farm tools with exception

(66-68)

of following bequest; to GEORGE W. TENNEY (no relationship
shown) one broad axe, two augers, one mason hammer, and one
stone pick; to dau. TURSEY, wife of Clark M. GOODWIN, one
cow worth $30 or price of cow to be pd. by sd. Peter and James
Barb within 1 yr. after testator's death.
      Teste., G. W. Ratcliff, Daniel C. Miller.
      Note. "Recorder appointed William P. McClain guardian ad
liten (sic) for Minerva Ann McClain, Elizabeth D. Mills, Peter
Mills, James E. Mills, Mary Jane Catherine Mills, infants and
heirs at law of Moses Barb deceased."
      Bk. A, pp. 106, 107.   /66/

      BRAKE, JACOB, Upshur County, W. Va., 5 Apr. 1867; 11 Oct.
1869.
      Children EDWARD HADDEN BRAKE, REBECCA FITZGERALD, ELIZA
BRAKE, GEORGE W. BRAKE, JACOB L. B. BRAKE, DAVID J. BRAKE, and
MARY POST, heirs of LEONARD J. BRAKE, deceased.   Jacob L. B.
Brake, ex.
      Testator bequeaths all personalty and home and 50 a. of
land to children EDWARD HADDEN BRAKE, REBECCA FITZGERALD, and
ELIZA BRAKE providing they care for testator during life and
provide him with "medicine, whiskey, food and clothing and all
comforts"; remainder of land to be sold after testator's death
for pmt. of debts and funeral expenses, any remaining proceeds
of sd. sale to be equally divided among children EDWARD H.,
GEORGE W., JACOB L. B., DAVID J. BRAKE, heirs of LEONARD J.
BRAKE, MARY POST, REBECCA FITZGERALD, and ELIZA BRAKE.
      Teste., J. Teter, William S. Gum, Joab Crites.
      Notation: David J. Brake objected to recording of will
on ground that testator was not of sound mind. Motion was
overruled.
      Bk. A, pp. 107, 108.   /67/

      FARNSWORTH, NATHANIEL, Buckhannon, Upshur County, W. Va.,
12 Sept. 1869; 13 Dec. 1869.
      Wife, SUSAN PERMELIA, son CALVIN E. FARNSWORTH.   No ex.
named.
      Testator bequeaths to wife SUSAN PERMELIA FARNSWORTH all
personalty and realty with exception of following bequest; to
son CALVIN E. FARNSWORTH, ½ of lot on Locust Street between
lots of J. D. Rapp and George H. Clark, testator having already given legatee title bond thereto.
      Teste., William C. Carper, George W. Balsley.
      Bk. A, p. 109.   /68/

      REGER, JOHN, Upshur County, W. Va., 14 Apr. 1870; 20 Aug.
1870.
      Wife MARGARET, MARY J. REGER (relationship not shown),
grandchildren LOUISA and CLINTON REGER, JEMIMA WOODS, ABRAM R.
McCOY (relationship not shown). Joshua Woods, ex.
      Testator desires pmt. of debts and funeral expenses; be-
queaths to wife MARGARET REGER all household and kitchen fur-

(69, 70)

niture, one "horse beast," and 3 cows, also two tracts of land
excepting 40 a. for lifetime; property not otherwise bequeathed to be sold in Oct. 1870, proceeds from sd. sale to be used
for pmt. of debts, any remainder thereof to sd. MARGARET REGER;
to MARY J. REGER, afsd. 40 a. of land; upon death of sd.
Margaret Reger 80 a. of sd. land to grandchildren LOUISA and
CLINTON REGER, also on death of sd. MARGARET /MARY/ J. REGER,
her 40 a. bequest to sd. grandchildren; to JEMIMA WOODS and
her heirs, remainder of lands bequeathed to Margaret Reger and
Mary J. Reger; to ABRAH R. McCOY, colt and saddle on condition
that he remain with testator or wife until he reaches 21; to
grandchildren (not named) equal division of proceeds from sale
of testator's land on east side of Buckhannon River.
    Teste., J. O. Wade, Jacob H. Burner.
    Bk. A, pp. 110, 111.   /69/

    PHILLIPS, HORACE A., Meade Tshp., Upshur County, W. Va.,
28 May 1870; 22 Aug. 1870.
    Wife SUSAN, bro. JOHN, sons GEORGE, SIMEON, ALBERT, BURTON,
GRANT, and DAVID PHILLIPS, daus. ANNA HOUGHTON, and ELECTA
PHILLIPS. No ex. named.
    Testator desires pmt. of legal debts; bequeaths to wife
SUSAN, 1/3 of realty and personalty for life use; to bro. JOHN
PHILLIPS, undivided share of land in Meade Tshp., formerly
owned by Uriah Phillips dec'd and purchased by him from heirs
of John Hunt; to sons GEORGE and ALBERT PHILLIPS, joint bequest of all remaining realty and personalty in Meade Tshp.,
when sd. Albert reaches age of 20; after death of sd. Susan
her property with certain exceptions to sd. GEORGE and ALBERT;
also to sd. GEORGE and ALBERT, one colt; to sd. ALBERT, a colt
to be "produced by the black mare in season of 1870"; sd.
George and Albert to pay following bequests: to dau. ANNA
HOUGHTON, $100 to be pd. May 28, 1878; to son SIMEON PHILLIPS,
$100 to be pd. May 28, 1879; to son BURTON PHILLIPS, $100 to
be pd. May 28, 1880; sd. Burton to have the privilege of rent-
ing and superintending home farm for 1/3 of products until
George and Albert take possession, 2/3 of products to be used
for maintenance of family; to dau. ELECTA /PHILLIPS/, $100 to
be pd. May 28, 1881; to son GRANT PHILLIPS, $100 to be pd. May
28, 1882; to son DAVID PHILLIPS, 8 a. of land between testator's
and sd. David's land.
    Teste., Festus Young, Adonijah Elmer, John J. Lemons.
    Bk. A, pp. 111, 112.   /70/

    BENNETT, DAVID, Upshur County, W. Va., 26 Jan. 1869;
10 Sept. 1870.
    Wife JANE G., daus. SARAH JANE and MARGARET BENNETT, son
JONATHAN BENNETT, other heirs, heirs of STUART BENNETT, heirs
of ELIZABETH ARMSTRONG, REBECCA TOWNSEND, JAMES N. BENNETT,
ABAGAIL CARPER, VIRGINIA CRICKARD, MARY BELL BENNETT, CHARLES
O. BENNETT, and COSBY C. BENNETT. Friend William H. Curry, ex.
    Testator desires pmt. of debts and funeral expenses; be-
queaths to wife JANE G. BENNETT "home place" on French Creek,

purchased from Archibald McCall, for life use, also all house-hold and kitchen furniture with provision that she share home with son JONATHAN BENNETT and daus. SARAH JANE and MARGARET BENNETT; to dau. SARAH JANE, 2 cows and one horse; to son JONATHAN, one "horse creature"; to dau. MARGARET, one "horse creature"; after afsd. bequests are made remaining personalty and realty to be sold and proceeds divided equally among "children and their heirs to wit"; to heirs of STUART BENNETT, $448; to heirs of ELIZA ARMSTRONG, $141; to REBECCA TOWNSEND, $250; to JAMES N. BENNETT, $400; to ABAGAIL CARPER, $180; to VIRGINIA CRICKARD, $200; son JONATHAN BENNETT to have privi-lege of taking meadow which was purchased from James N. Bennett at appraisement value, also farming utensils at appraisement value; upon death of sd. Jane G. Bennett, farm and mansion house to sd. JONATHAN BENNETT with provision that he pay testa-tor's dau. SARAH J. BENNETT, $1,000; sd. Jonathan also to pay to children of William M. Bennett as follows: to MARY BELL BENNETT, $300; to CHARLES O. BENNETT, $400; to COSBY C. BENNETT, $300; sd. bequests to be pd. when age of 21 is reached, also to sd. MARY BELL and COSBY C., when they reach the age of 18, one good horse, saddle, and bridle, the same bequest to sd. CHARLES O., when he reaches 20.
    Teste., William H. Curry, J. N. Curry.
    Codicil, 16 Mar. 1870.
    Authorizes ex. to sell any and all unsold land in posses-sion of testator at time of death.
    Teste., John C. Hull, Harvey S. Pritt, W. H. Curry.
    Bk. A, pp. 113-115. /71/

    MOORE, CHESLEY K., Upshur County, W. Va., 29 Nov. 1870; 27 Dec. 1870.
    Wife ELIZA. Eliza Moore, ex.
    Testator desires pmt. of just debts; bequeaths to wife ELIZA MOORE, all realty and personalty.
    Teste., Valentine Strader, John J. Reger.
    Bk. A, p. 115. /72/

    GIBSON, ENOCH, Upshur County, W. Va., 8 Apr. 1869; 16 Feb. 1871.
    Wife /MARGARET/, son OVID T. GIBSON, grandson CHARLES J. LAWHORN. No ex. named.
    Testator desires pmt. of debts and funeral expenses; be-queaths to wife /MARGARET/, 1/3 of estate, sd. share upon her death to son OVID T. GIBSON; to grandson CHARLES J. LAWHORN, one bed and one cow; remainder of estate to sd. son OVID T.
    Teste., Granville P. Shreve, Charles B. Shreve, J. B. Shreve.
    Bk. A, pp. 116, 117. /73/

HEAVNER, NATHAN, Upshur County, W. Va., 3 Apr. 1871;
4 May 1871.
    Wife S. J. HEAVNER. Gideon M. Heavner, ex.
    Testator desires pmt. of debts and funeral expenses; be-
queaths to wife S. J. HEAVNER all realty and personalty.
    Teste., James J. Kiddy, Martin E. Shreves.
    Bk. A, p. 117.   /74/

    PAUGH, WILLIAM, Upshur County, W. Va., 12 Mar. 1871;
17 May 1871.
    Wife MARY, dau. CATHERINE PAUGH, grandsons CLARENCE P.
WHITE and JAMES E. WHITE, grdau. CATHERINE WHITE. No ex.
named.
    Testator desires pmt. of debts and funeral expenses; be-
queaths to wife MARY PAUGH all realty and personalty for life
use; on death of sd. Mary White all realty and personalty to
dau. CATHERINE PAUGH; on death of sd. Catherine Paugh property
to her heirs or, if she die without issue to be devised as
follows: to grandson JAMES E. WHITE, ½ of proceeds of sd.
estate; to grandson CLARENCE P. WHITE, ¼ of sd. estate; to
grdau. CATHERINE WHITE, ¼ of sd. estate; also bequeaths to
grandson CLARENCE WHITE, $5 when he reaches 21 yrs. of age;
also to grdau. CATHERINE WHITE, $5 when she reaches 21 yrs.
of age.
    Teste., O. B. Loudin, John Ireland, W. B. Loudin.
    Bk. A, p. 118.   /75/

    SEXTON, A/UGUSTUS/ W., Meade Tshp., Upshur County, W. Va.,
7 Apr. 1870; 3 June 1871.
    Wife ANNE L., sons FREEMAN S., and WORTHINGTON SEXTON,
dau. ALMYRA E. SEXTON, other heirs (relationship not shown)
LOUISA A. A. HAYS, LOUISA ELLEN SILCOTT. No ex. named.
    Testator bequeaths to ANNE L. SEXTON "wife with whom I
have lived in wedlock more than half a century" all realty and
personalty with right to sell as she desires; to sons FREEMAN
S. SEXTON and WORTHINGTON L. SEXTON, prior gifts; after death
of sd. wife Anne L. Sexton property remaining in her possession
to be distributed "among other heirs" LOUISA A. A. HAYS,
ALMYRA E. SEXTON, and LOUISA ELLEN SILCOTT, dau. ALMYRA to
reside with sd. Anne L. during her lifetime and to have prefer-
ence in distribution of home, also to share equally in distribution of estate and prior deed to half of 34 a. "east of the
road leading to Centerville and near the school house" not to
be included in estate.
    Teste., Loyal Young, M. P. Young.
    Bk. A, pp. 119, 120.   /76/

    LOUDIN, THOMAS, Upshur County, W. Va., 16 June 1870;
19 Sept. 1871.
    Daus. KATHARINE TETER, JULIA DAWSON, MARGARET HYRE,
ELIZABETH JENNING, and MARIA GREEN. Sons John M., and William
Loudin, exs.
    Testator desires pmt. of funeral expenses for self and
wife (not named) and debts; exs. to sell realty and personalty

and bequests to be pd. from proceeds thereof; bequeaths to daus. KATHARINE TETER, JULIA DAWSON, MARGARET HYRE, and ELIZA-BETH JENNING equal shares of sd. proceeds of sd. sale in addition to prior gifts of $50 each; to dau. MARIA GREEN, stove "and appurtenances" and prior gift of 50 a. of land.
    Teste., J. W. Reger, Nathan Rexroad.
    Bk. A, pp. 120, 121. /77/

JONES, NELSON, Washington Tshp., Upshur County, W. Va., 24 Apr. 1871; 23 Sept. 1871.
    Wife MARTHA JANE, dau. FRANCIS CORA, 4 children not named. Granville Strader, ex.
    Testator bequeaths to wife MARTHA JANE, 1 mare and colt, 2 cows, 5 sheep, 2 hogs, household and kitchen furniture, also any remaining personalty after pmt. of debts and funeral expenses, also possession of realty until children reach legal age providing she remain a widow; when children have all reached legal age realty to be equally divided "between 5 children of testator"; to dau. FRANCIS CORA, $50 in addition to share in afsd. bequest.
    Teste., G. D. Marple, G. Strader.
    Bk. A, p. 122. /78/

TALLMAN, BENNY, Washington Tshp., Upshur County, W. Va., 10 Jan. 1869; 29 Nov. 1871.
    Wife SOPHRONIA, dau. NANCY E. TALLMAN, son CYRUS G. TALLMAN, grdau. LUELLA TALLMAN. Y. Abner Norvell and Sophronia Tallman, exs.
    Testator desires pmt. of debts and funeral expenses; bequeaths to wife SOPHRONIA TALLMAN all realty and personalty for life or widowhood; upon death of sd. Sophronia or in event of her remarriage, realty to be sold by ex. and proceeds distributed as follows: to grdau. LOUELLA TALLMAN, $50; remainder of proceeds to be equally divided between dau. NANCY E. TALLMAN of Shelby County, "Elinois" and son CYRUS G. TALLMAN "supposed to be living in Indiana."
    No witnesses. Proven by Noah B. Wamsley, R. G. H. Benton.
    Bk. A, pp. 123, 124. /79/

TENNEY, PETER SR., Washington Tshp., Upshur County, W. Va., 28 Aug. 1871; 30 Nov. 1871.
    Wife LABANY, sons SANDUSKY, PETER JR., GEORGE A., and RUFUS TENNEY, daus. BANEY ANN CURRENCE, BATHANEY JANE READ, and SARAH CATHERINE /TENNEY/, other heirs not named. No ex. named.
    Testator desires pmt. of debts and funeral expenses; bequeaths to wife LABANY TENNEY, home farm for life use with privilege of selling 25 a. "along the line of Jonathan Tenney's land," proceeds of sd. sale to be divided among children and heirs at law of testator; also ½ of household and kitchen furniture, farm implements, and live stock; to son SANDUSKY TENNEY, ½ of sd. furniture, implements, and stock; sd. Labany and Sandusky are to give to testator's dau. SARAH CATHERINE /TENNEY/,

1 cow, 4 sheep, 1 bed and bedding, also share in afsd. sale proceeds when she reaches 21; upon death of sd. Labany, home farm to son SANDUSKY TENNEY; to sons GEORGE A. TENNEY and RUFUS TENNEY, in addition to afsd. bequest, 1 horse for which they are to pay estate $15 each; to dau. BANEY ANN CURRENCE, in addition to afsd. bequest, $10; to dau. BATHANEY JANE READ, in addition to afsd. bequest, $10.

    Teste., Noah B. Wamsley, G. D. Marple.
    Codicil, 31 Aug. 1871.
    PETER TENNEY JR. added to list of heirs.
    Teste., N. B. Wamsley, Nicholas Ours, Jr.
    Bk. A, pp. 124-126.   /80/

    GRIMM, JOHN, Upshur County, W. Va., 23 Feb. 1872; 1 Apr. 1872.

    Wife EM, sons ABRAM and ISAAC H. GRIMM. Valentine Hinkle, ex.

    Testator desires pmt. of debts and funeral expenses; bequeaths to wife EM GRIMM household and kitchen furniture, all personalty and maintenance from realty; to sons ABRAM and ISAAC H. GRIMM, equal division of realty with provision that they support sd. Em.

    Teste., John N. Johnson, Granville Dean.
    Bk. A, p. 127.   /81/

    HODGES, JOHN R., Upshur County, W. Va., June 1867; 18 May 1872.

    Wife ELIZABETH W., sons JOHN HENRY, JAMES F., OSCAR F., GEORGE N., THEOPHILUS F., and BUSHROD B. HODGES; daus. SARAH JANE /KIDD/, LUCY C. SHACKLEFORD, MARTHA E. /CORDER/, MILDRED S., and MALINDA A. HODGES. Elizabeth W. Hodges, ex.

    Testator desires pmt. of debts and funeral expenses from sale of personalty; bequeaths to wife ELIZABETH W. HODGES, 1 horse, 2 cows, household and kitchen furniture and home farm for life use; sd. Elizabeth, with consent of 2/3 of children of legal age may sell sd. realty and retain proceeds thereof for her use; any other property to be distributed as follows: to son JOHN HENRY HODGES, $200 in addition to prior gift of $100; to dau. SARAH JANE /KIDD/, $200 in addition to prior gift of $100; to dau. LUCY C. SHACKLEFORD, $200 in addition to prior gift of $100; to son JAMES F. HODGES, $200 in addition to prior gift of $100; to son OSCAR F. HODGES, $300 when he reaches 21 yrs.; to dau. MARTHA E. HODGES, $300 and interest thereon from the time she was 21 until pd.; upon death of sd. Elizabeth all property remaining in her hands to be sold and the proceeds therefrom equally divided among all children; to children MILDRED S. HODGES, GEORGE N. HODGES, THEOPHILUS F. HODGES, MALINDA A. HODGES, and BUSHROD B. HODGES, $300 each when they reach the age of 21; to the PROTESTANT METHODIST CHURCH "or any other church selected by Elizabeth Hodges" $100 to be used in "building a place of public worship in the neighborhood in which she may reside providing a similar amount has

(82-84)

not been given by the testator during his life"; if, after
afsd. bequests are pd., any money or bonds remain then sd.
ELIZABETH is to receive $1,000 in money or bonds.
     Teste., W. G. Harper, Henry Neff.
     Codicil, 4 Feb. 1871.
     Rescinds provision in will giving $300 each to Sarah Jane
Kidd, John Henry Hodges, Lucy Shackleford, Martha E. Corder,
and Oscar F. Hodges, testator having already given to John
Henry, Sarah Jane, Lucy and Martha E., $400 each and to Oscar
F., and James F., $200; bequeaths to OSCAR F., furniture val-
ued at $100; to JAMES F., $100 and furniture valued at $100;
to children not yet of legal age, $100 each in addition to be-
quests provided in will; to wife ELIZABETH, all remaining
personalty.
     Teste., Henry Neff, O. B. Loudin, William Frymyre.
     Bk. A, pp. 128-131.   /82/

     BURR, JOHN J., Upshur County, W. Va., 11 Oct. 1866; 21
June 1872.
     Wife AMY W., daus. LOUISA BASSEL and MARY S. RIDGWAY;
grandson OLEN B. SQUIRE, grdau. ANN ELIZABETH LORENTZ. Bro.
Elbrige G. Burr, ex.
     Testator desires pmt. of debts and funeral expenses; be-
queaths to wife AMY W., $2,000; remainder of estate to daus.
and heirs of deceased daus., namely: to dau. LOUISA, wife of
Daniel BASSEL, ¼ of estate; to dau. MARY S., wife of C. F.
RIDGWAY, ¼ of estate; to grandson OLEN B. SQUIRE, son of testator's deceased dau. Amelia Squire, ¼ of estate; to grandau.
ANN ELIZABETH LORENTZ, dau. of testator's deceased dau. Ann
Elizabeth Lorentz, ¼ of estate; bequests to sd. Olen B. Squire
and Ann Elizabeth Lorentz to be pd. when they reach age of 25
with exception of ex. expenditures for maintenance and education; in case of death of sd. Olen B. Squire or Ann Elizabeth
Lorentz before they reach 25 then equal division of property
among other legatees.
     Teste., Henry Simpson, William C. Carper.
     Bk. A, pp. 131, 132.
     Renunciation, 5 July 1872.
     Amy W. Burr, legatee in preceding will of John J. Burr
appeared in court and renounced the sd. will and claimed her
distributive share of the estate.
     Bk. A, p. 133.   /83/

     BRADY, THOMAS, Upshur County, W. Va., 3 Jan. 1873; Feb.
term, 1873.
     Wife CATHARINE BRANEN BRADY. No ex. named.
     Testator bequeaths all realty and personalty to wife
CATHARINE BRANEN BRADY with full authority to dispose of property by sale or gift; "this has not been done to cheat children but to keep them from cheating her."
     Teste., Henry Cain, John Cunningham.
     Bk. A, p. 134.   /84/

QUEEN, LEVI H., Upshur County, W. Va., 7 Feb. 1873;
Apr. term, 1873.
Sons JONATHAN L., ANTHONY G., PETER T. L., A. J., and
JOHN W. QUEEN, dau. LUCINDA SMITH, grdaus. SARAH /WHITE7
RINEHEART and SARAH M. QUEEN, grandsons HARRISON H. and
LLOYD QUEEN. Son John W. Queen, ex.
Testator desires pmt. of debts and funeral expenses; be-
queaths to son JONATHAN L. QUEEN, $75; to son ANTHONY G.
QUEEN, $10; to son PETER T. L. QUEEN, $15; to son A. J. QUEEN,
$11; to dau. LUCINDA SMITH, $15; to grdau. SARAH /WHITE7
RINEHEART, $15; to grandson HARRISON H. QUEEN, son of Washington
Queen, deceased, $5; to grdau. SARAH M. QUEEN, sister of sd.
Harrison H., $5; to grandson LLOYD QUEEN, bro. of sd. Harrison
H., $5; sd. legacies to be pd. out of $500 loaned by testator
to John Post; to son JOHN W. QUEEN, remainder of sd. $500 after
pmt. of legacies.
Teste., J. W. Weaver, John Kee, Jacob Lorentz.
Bk. A, pp. 134, 135.   /85/

HUFFMAN, HENRY L., Upshur County, W. Va., 12 May 1873;
Aug. term, 1873.
Wife SUSAN, children SEDRICK LEE, JANE, HENRY THOMAS
and unnamed infant son. Sampson Huffman, ex.
Testator bequeaths to wife SUSAN HUFFMAN, all household
and kitchen furniture; to children SEDRICK LEE, JANE, HENRY
THOMAS, and unnamed infant son, remainder of property con-
sisting of 1 cow and calf, 3 sheep and 5 hogs; Sampson Huffman
to be appointed guardian for sd. children.
Teste., William Griffeth (his mark), D. P. Huffman.
Bk. A, pp. 135, 136.
Renunciation. 20 Aug. 1873.
SUSAN HUFFMAN, widow of HENRY L. HUFFMAN renounces pro-
visions of will of sd. Henry L., and makes widow's claim to
estate.
Teste., H. D. Clark.
Bk. A, p. 136.   /86/

MATHENY, ANNA, Washington District, Upshur County, W. Va.,
24 May 1873; 9 Feb. 1874.
Daus., CATHARINE REED, MARY A. HEARTMAN, REBECCA R.
COURTNEY, ELIZATH M. SIMONS, and SARAH M. FOSTER, JACOB REED
(relationship not shown). Jacob Reed, ex.
Testatrix bequeaths to dau. CATHARINE REED, 1 bed and
bedding, 1 breakfast table, 1 clock, and 1 tea kettle; to
dau. MARY A. HEARTMAN, 1 bedstead, bed and bedding, 1 small
skillet and lid;to dau. REBECCA R. COURTNEY, 1 side saddle;
to dau. ELIZATH M. SIMONS, 1 bed and bedding, 1 chest, 1 oven
and lid, 1 looking glass; to dau. SARAH M. FOSTER, 1 low bedstead and bedding, 1 cupboard, and 1 large kettle; to JACOB
REED, 1 cow valued at $30, sd. Jacob Reed to see that testatrix
is "decently buried"; remainder of property to be equally divided among afsd. daus.
Teste., G. W. Tenney, G. D. Marple.
Bk. A, p. 137.   /87/

(88, 89)

SEXTON, WILLIAM, Upshur County, W. Va., 18 Nov. 1873; 9
Feb. 1874.
Wife SARAH A., daus., SARAH E., and AMY A. SEXTON.   Son
George A. Sexton, ex.
Testator desires ex. to sell, as soon as possible, home
farm except ¼ a., and testators 2/6 interest in a 720 a. tract
in Gilmer County, proceeds therefrom to be used for pmt. of
debts and a note of $200 executed by testator's son William A.
Sexton with testator as surety and held by the National Exchange Bank at Weston; remainder of proceeds to be placed on
interest and sd. interest to be pd. annually to testator's wife
SARAH A. SEXTON; also to sd. SARAH, ¼ a. of home farm "east
side of road where the barn stands"; also to sd. SARAH, all
household goods, livestock, farm crops and implements; sd.
Sarah is to "make a home" for testator's daus. SARAH E., and
AMY A. SEXTON until they marry and at that time provide for
them "the same or equivalent outfits as the other children received at their marriages"; upon death of sd. Sarah A., household and farming equipment to be sold and the proceeds divided
equally among children (not named); to dau. SARAH E. SEXTON,
1 horse colt; to dau. AMY A. SEXTON, 1 horse when she reaches
legal age, sd. legacy to be provided by sd. Sarah A. Sexton.
Teste., A. M. Poundstone, Valentine Strader.
Bk. A, pp. 140-142.
Renunciation, 6 Feb., 1875.
SARAH A. SEXTON, widow of WILLIAM SEXTON renounces provisions made for her in the will of sd. William Sexton.
Teste., Daniel Cutright, J.P.
Bk. A, pp. 162, 163.   /88/

McNULTY, CLARK W., Upshur County, W. Va., 18 Oct. 1873;
9 Feb. 1874.
Wife CATHARINE, children MARGARET ROHRBOUGH, WILLIAM A.
McNULTY, and VIRGINIA L. SEXTON. Son William A. McNulty and
son-in-law Marshall L. Rohrbough, exs.
Testator desires pmt. of debts from sale of realty and
personalty, not otherwise bequeathed, sd. sale to be made
within 18 mos. after testator's death; to wife CATHARINE
McNULTY, interest of $3,000 to be invested from proceeds of
sd. sale, interest to be pd. annually; also to sd. CATHARINE,
all household "goods and furniture," mare and buggy, all rents
and profits from estate from time of testator's death until it
is sold; remainder of estate to be equally divided among children MARGARET ROHRBOUGH, WILLIAM A. McNULTY, and VIRGINIA L.
SEXTON; upon death of sd. Catharine, sd. bequest of $3,000 to
be equally divided among sd. children.
Teste., Jacob Waugh, W. G. L. Totten, A. M. Poundstone.
Bk. A, pp. 138, 139.   /89/

(90-92)

CRABTREE, WILLIAM, Muskingum County, Ohio, 7 Dec. 1867;
Upshur County, W. Va., 10 Feb. 1874.
Wife SARAH, sons SAMUEL, EDWARD, JULIUS, JOHN, JAMES,
daus. MARY KELLY, HANNAH, son-in-law NATHAN KELLY. F. A.
Seborn of Zanesville, Ohio, ex.
Testator desires pmt. of debts; bequeaths to wife SARAH
CRABTREE, life use and profit from realty and personalty;
after death of sd. Sarah,1/7 of property to son SAMUEL; to
son EDWARD, 1/7 of property; to son JULIUS, 1/7 of property;
to son JOHN, 1/7 of property; to NATHAN KELLY and his heirs
as trustee for son JAMES and his heirs, 1/7 of property; to
dau. MARY /KELLY/ and heirs, 1/7 of property; to children of
testator's dau. HANNAH and their heirs, 1/7 of property; division of estate to be based on statement in hands of F. A.
Seborn and all prior gifts and debts owed by legatees to testator to be considered in distribution.
Teste., John C. Davy, Samuel Chapman.
Bk. A, pp. 143-146. /90/

SEXTON, LUCINDA, Meade District, Upshur County, W. Va.,
22 Sept. 1873; 26 Feb. 1874.
Daus. ROSA M., MARY EVA, and LIBBIE GRAY SEXTON. Father,
Ebenezer Leonard, ex.
Testatrix desires pmt. of debts and funeral expenses
from estate; all personalty to be sold and equal division made
to daus., ROSA M., MARY EVA, and LIBBIE GRAY SEXTON; 60 a. of
land nr. Meadville on French Creek which was conveyed to testatrix's deceased husband, James Sexton, by George See, to be
sold within 3 yrs. after death of testatrix and to be equally
divided among afsd. daus.
Teste., C. S. Haynes, L. Carper, A. Clark.
Bk. A, pp. 146, 147. /91/

HUMPHREY, MERRYWETHER T., Upshur County, W. Va., 2 Oct. 1873;
4 Apr. 1874.
Wife SUSAN, daus. MINERVA R. FRETWELL and MELISSA M.
HODGES, sons ROBERT R., JAMES BROKENBOROUGH, and ALEXANDER
LEVINESTON HUMPHREY. Son Robert R. Humphrey, ex.
Testator desires pmt. of debts and funeral expenses from
personalty; bequeaths to wife SUSAN all realty consisting of
102 a. on Little Sand Run deeded to testator by James N. Jackson
and Watson Westfall, also all personalty after pmt. of debts;
sd. bequest to be shared with dau. MINERVA R. FRETWELL as long
as she remains with sd. Susan; at death of sd. Susan, realty and
personalty to be sold and proceeds to be distributed equally
among children of testator ROBERT R. HUMPHREY, JAMES BROKENBOROUG:
HUMPHREY, ALEXANDER LEVINESTON HUMPHREY, MELISSA M. HODGES, and
sd. Minerva R. Fretwell.
Teste., Watson Westfall, Joseph Houser, George W.
ratcliff.
Bk. A, pp. 147, 148. /92/

(93-95)

SMITH, CHRISTAIN, Upshur County, W. Va., 14 Feb. 1872; 21 Apr. 1874.
Wife JANE, sons PERRY D., and JOSEPH C., dau. MARTHA E. PARKER. No ex. named.
Testator desires pmt. of debts and funeral expenses; bequeaths to wife JANE SMITH all personalty with provision that she pay following bequests: son PERRY D., "if his mind should prove capable" a good English education; son JOSEPH C., "a good complete English education"; to dau. MARTHA E. PARKER $200 in addition to prior gifts.
Teste., Jacob Waugh, Philip F. Pinnell, Levi Leonard, Thos. J. Farnsworth.
Bk. A, pp. 150, 151.   /93/

CUTRIGHT, CASANNA, Upshur County, W. Va., 25 Feb. 1874; Apr. term, 1874.
Sons THAMER and MARSHALL CUTRIGHT. No ex. named.
Testator desires that Elizah Stansberry provide decent burial and be pd. "according to the contract that is written between us"; bequeaths to son THAMER CUTRIGHT, $20; remainder of estate to son MARSHALL CUTRIGHT.
Teste., Elizah Stansberry, G. D. Marple.
Bk. A, pp. 149, 150.   /94/

JONES, ANNE S., Frederick County, Va., 17 Dec. 1844; Upshur County, W. Va., 9 June 1874.
Friend, HENRY O. MIDDLETON, servant MARY ANN. Henry O. Middleton, ex.
Testatrix desires pmt. of debts; bequeaths to friend HENRY O. MIDDLETON, all realty and personalty that testatrix may inherit; to servant MARY ANN, $20 annually to be pd. quarterly by ex. "as a testimony and sense of her obedience and kindness to me during life"; ex. to dispose of wearing apparel as he may see fit.
Teste., H. B. Hall, William Allen.
Bk. A, p. 152.   /95/
Reacknowledgment of will, 18 Apr. 1855.
Teste., Richard L. Brown, Wm. M. Buckner, O. D. Brown.

QUEEN, MARTHA, Upshur County, W. Va., 18 Mar. 1874; June term, 1874.
Daus. DEBORAH STOUT, REBECCA QUEEN, son THOMAS CLARK. David T. Tolbert, ex.
Testatrix desires pmt. of debts and funeral expenses and purchase of grave stones for herself and Isaac Clark not to cost more than $50; bequeaths to youngest dau. DEBORAH STOUT all remaining personalty and realty, Jesse G. Norman to be appointed guardian of sd. Deborah.
Teste., L. L. D. Peters, Elvira Starcher, Jacob Starcher.
Codicil, n.d.
Provision for grave stones changed to $20; to dau. REBECCA QUEEN, "one white back cow," son THOMAS CLARK, and

(96-98)

sd. REBECCA having received father's estate, no further pro-
vision is made for them.
Teste:, L. L. D. Peters, J. G. Norman.
Bk. A, pp. 153, 154.   /96/

YOUNG, GILBERT, Upshur County, W. Va., 24 Apr. 1874;
Aug. term, 1874.
Wife AMMYLLIS, daus. MARGARET BROWN, ESTELLA PHILLIPS,
and MARTHA PAGE. No ex. named.
Testator desires settlement of a claim held by George
Phillips amounting to $200, settlement to be made with
J. J. Morgan and Festus Young and to consist of a quantity
of land sufficient to satisfy claim "beginning at the south
west corner adjoining lands of James Mills /Miles/ and
Harrison Wingrove and running to include sd. George Phillips
improvement"; bequeaths to wife AMMYLLIS remainder of realty
and personalty for life; at death of sd. Ammyllis property
to be equally divided among daus. MARGARET BROWN, ESTELLA
PHILLIPS, and MARTHA PAGE; should sd. Estella die childless,
her share to heirs of sd. Margaret and Martha.
Teste., Festus Young, J. J. Morgan.
Bk. A, pp. 154, 155.   /97/

BASTABLE, A. M., Upshur County, W. Va., 1 Jan. 1874;
11 Sept. 1874.
Wife, JANE, dau. MAY BASTABLE, son MILTON W. BASTABLE.
Wife Jane Bastable, ex.
Testator desires pmt. of debts and funeral expenses;
bequeaths to wife JANE BASTABLE, home property in Buckhannon
or $2,750, also $1,500 for her own use, also $500 to be used
in caring for testator's children May and Milton W. Bastable,
also household and kitchen furniture with exception of piano,
also 1 cow, wheat and bacon, also 1/3 of proceeds from sale
of property in Culpepper County, Va., with provision that she
is to clothe and board sd. children; to dau. MAY BASTABLE,
$50 and the piano, also ¼ or remainder of estate in West
Virginia, also her share in sd. Culpepper County property, also
her share of bonds to be selected by sd. Jane Bastable; to
son MILTON W. BASTABLE, $100 and share in Va. property as set
forth in preceding bequest; to A. N. BASTABLE, and JAMES
BASTABLE (relationship not shown), ¼ interest each in West
Virginia property, also their share of bonds; testator owns
410 a. of land 2 mi. east of Brandy Station, Culpepper County,
Virginia, purchased in 1864 from James O. Harris of Atlanta,
Ga., sd. land now being in litigation in the circuit court in
Culpepper County, if decision is made for testator then distribution of sd. property to be made as set forth in preced-
ing bequests; if home property is sold funds to be placed in
estate for general distribution; notes owed at time will made
are as follows: Exchange Bank at Weston, $300; J. G. Bastable,
$250 and interest; A. N. Bastable, $125 and interest; Jane
Bastable, $158 and interest.
Teste., David T. Peterson, Anthony Reger, G. Austin Newlon.
Bk. A, pp. 156-158.   /98/

(99-102)

MATHERS, LUCINDA J., Buckhannon, Upshur County, W. Va., 20 Apr. 1874; 28 Sept. 1874.
     Son GEORGE E. MATHERS. Joseph R. Mathers, ex.
     Testatrix bequeaths to son GEORGE E. MATHERS all personalty and realty.
     Teste., Joseph Ward, George W. Stewart.
     Bk. A, pp. 158, 159.   /99/

CUTRIGHT, JACOB, Upshur County, W. Va., 21 June 1870; 16 Oct. 1874.
     Wife ELIZABETH, sons GEORGE, ELMER, CLARK, THEODORE, and DEXTER W. CUTRIGHT, daus. NAOMI CUTRIGHT, ISABELLA CUTRIGHT, SUSAN PHILLIPS, and ANN GOODWIN. Theodore Cutright, ex.
     Testator desires pmt. of debts and funeral expenses; bequeaths to wife ELIZABETH CUTRIGHT, 1 mare, 1 cow, 2 beds, and bedding, "the cupboard with its usual contents," all cooking utensils and her own sidesaddle and bridle; to son GEORGE CUTRIGHT, $20 and prior gift of land; to son ELMER CUTRIGHT, $20 and prior gift of land; to son CLARK CUTRIGHT, $20 and prior gifts; to daus. NAOMI CUTRIGHT, ISABELLA CUTRIGHT, SUSAN, wife of Horace PHILLIPS, and ANN, wife of Elijah GOODWIN, each $\frac{1}{4}$ of proceeds of sale of personalty after bequests are made and $100 from testator's sons Theodore and Dexter W., to sons THEODORE and DEXTER W. CUTRIGHT, equal division of remainder of home farm with provision that they care for testator's wife Elizabeth and that sd. Theodore pay to Naomi Cutright and Ann Goodwin, $100 each, and that sd. Dexter W., pay to Isabella Cutright and Susan Phillips $100 each.
     Teste., Watson Westfall, Jasper N. Westfall, Austin Loudin.
     Bk. A, pp. 159-161.   /100/

YOUNG, EARLE E., Upshur County, W. Va., 26 July 1873; 8 Dec. 1874.
     Wife, MARY E. No ex. named.
     Testator bequeaths to wife MARY E. YOUNG, all realty and personality.
     Teste., Elias S. Bronson, James M. Sharpes.
     Bk. A, p. 162.   /101/

SMITH, J. L. B., Upshur County, W. Va., 18 Jan. 1875; 18 Mar. 1875.
     Wife BERSHEBA M., son ESKER T. SMITH. No ex. named.
     Testator desires pmt. of debts; bequeaths to wife BERSHEBA M. SMITH, all realty and personalty until son ESKER T. SMITH reaches legal age, when he is to share equally in realty; sd. Bersheba to care for testator's father and mother (not named).
     Teste., William H. Curry, Milton D. Mearns.
     Bk. A, p. 163.   /102/

OWENS, PATRICK, Upshur County, W. Va., 28 Apr. 1873;
13 Apr. 1875.
Wife not named, son THOMAS OWENS, dau. MARY OWENS. No
ex. named.
Testator bequeaths to dau. MARY OWENS, 1 heifer and 3
sheep; to son THOMAS OWENS, remainder of personalty and all
realty with provision that he care for testator's wife (not
named) during her lifetime; if sd. Thomas does not carry out
obligations, then testator's wife may claim 1/3 of realty, 1
cow, 1 colt, and ½ of sheep for life use; sd. realty to sd.
Thomas on death of testator's wife.
Teste., Michael Walsh, Edward Gormeley.
Bk. A, p. 164.   /103/

HEAVNER, MARY E., Widow of T. S. Heavner, Buckhannon,
Upshur County, W. Va., 27 July 1874; 4 Aug. 1875.
Dau. LENORAH A. HEAVNER, mother SUSANNAH P. FARNSWORTH,
sisters CATHARINE PINNELL and SARAH J. FREY. Bro. Thomas J.
Farnsworth and bro.-in-law John M. Pinnell, exs.
Testatrix desires pmt. of funeral expenses and purchase
of tombstone for grave; bequeaths to only dau. LENORAH A.
HEAVNER, all realty and personalty when she reaches legal
age, or upon her marriage, or when "guardian deems it proper
to deliver same"; to mother SUSANNAH P. FARNSWORTH all
interest accruing on realty and personalty, any remaining at
time of Susannah A. Farnsworth's death to sd. Lenorah A.
Heavner; if sd. Lenorah A. Heavner dies without issue, property to testatrix's sisters CATHARINE L. PINNELL and SARAH J.
FREY.
Teste., E. P. Westfall, Henry F. Westfall.
Bk. A, pp. 165, 166.   /104/

O'CONNER, JAMES, Upshur County, W. Va., 7 Apr. 1875;
13 Sept. 1875.
Wife BRIDGET, dau. MARY ELLEN O'CONNER. No ex. named.
Testator bequeaths to wife BRIDGET O'CONNER, life use of
realty and personalty, upon her death sd. property to dau.
MARY ELLEN O'CONNER; in case sd. Mary Ellen dies without heirs
then property "to pass over to Church."
Teste., Myles King, Michael Fitzpatrick.
Bk. A, p. 167.   /105/

RICE, JOTHAM, Upshur County, W. Va., 19 Nov. 1870; 20
Sept. 1875.
Sons MARTIN M. and LEWIS RICE, daus. SARAH ANN and
MARGARET CATHARINE RICE. Martin M. Rice, ex.
Testator desires pmt. of debts and funeral expenses; bequeaths to son LEWIS RICE, all of home place except a certain
boundary adjoining John Teter's land, also 100 a. on Flat Run;
to son MARTIN M., 200 a. adjoining sd. Lewis' 100 a. bequest;
to dau. SARAH ANN RICE, ½ of 375 a. tract of land, but if she
dies without issue, sd. tract to sd. Lewis Rice; to dau. MARGARET

(106-109)

CATHARINE RICE, remaining ½ of sd. tract, sd. Margaret to live
with sd. Lewis who is to inherit if she dies without issue; in
event of sd. Margaret's marriage, Lewis is to pay her $200; if
sd. Margaret prefers to live with sd. Martin, then he is to inherit; all remaining realty and personalty to son MARTIN RICE.
   Teste., James Long, George A. Long.
   Bk. A, pp. 168, 169.   /106/

   SIMON, ELIAS, Upshur County, W. Va., 18 Apr. 1873; 11 Oct.
1875.
   Wife NANCY, son LEONARD R. SIMON, daus. VIRGINIA HERDMAN,
and ANZINA MAXWELL, grdau. NANCY ALMIRA YOUNG. John B. Simon
and Leonard R. Simon, exs.
   Testator bequeaths to youngest son LEONARD R. SIMON home
farm and all personalty not otherwise bequeathed with provision that he care for testator's wife NANCY SIMON and pay following bequests: to testator's daus. VIRGINIA HERDMAN and
ANZINA MAXWELL, $5 each; to grdau. NANCY ALMIRA YOUNG, 1 cow.
   Teste., C. S. Haynes, J. B. Simon.
   Bk. A, pp. 169, 170.   /107/

   BOLDEN, CHARLES W., Buckhannon, Upshur County, W. Va., 26
Nov. 1875; 6 Dec. 1875.
   Mother, not named. TRUSTEES OF METHODIST EPISCOPAL CHURCH.
James A. Davis, ex.
   Testator desires pmt. of debts and funeral expenses from
sale of personalty; desires sale of house and lot in Buckhannon
and collection of $44.43 from James A. Davis; bequeaths to
trustees of METHODIST EPISCOPAL CHURCH, $50 to be applied to
the construction of "a place of Religious worship for the benefit of the colored people of Buckhannon"; remainder of estate
to mother (not named).
   Teste., Jacob Waugh, James A. Davis, Henry Mumphord.
   Bk. A, pp. 171, 172.   /108/

   TENNEY, PHILO, Upshur County, W. Va., 22 Jan. 1876; 14
Feb. 1876.
   Wife REBECCA. No ex. named.
   Testator desires pmt. of debts; bequeaths to wife REBECCA
TENNEY, 1 cow, all household and kitchen furniture, and remain-
der of "purchase-money" for land sold to James M. Black.
   Teste., Nicholas Ours, Theo. Cutright, M. Boyles.
   Bk. A. p. 174.   /109/

   ROHRBOUGH, BENJAMIN, Upshur County, W. Va., 28 Jan. 1873;
21 Feb. 1876.
   Wife LYDIA, sons JOHN H., and heirs of DAVID B. ROHRBOUGH,
daus. PERMELIA E. HERNDON, RACHEL R. MURRELL, MARY S. CALHOUN,
and CATHARINE L. WEAVER. David B. Rohrbough, ox.
   Testator desires pmt. of debts and funeral expenses; bequeaths to wife LYDIA ROHRBOUGH, 1/3 of realty, also 1 cow,

(110, 111)

1 horse, life use of household and kitchen furniture, also
$100, also sewing machine; remaining realty to son DAVID B.
ROHRBOUGH who is to provide home for sd. Lydia and receive
her property upon her death with exception of ½ of bedding
which sd. Lydia may dispose of as she sees fit; sd. David is
to pay following bequests: to heirs of testator's son JOHN
H. ROHRBOUGH, $250; to dau. PERMELIA E. HERDON, $200; to
dau. RACHEL R. MURRELL, $300; to dau. MARY S. CALHOUN, $100;
to dau. CATHARINE L. WEAVER, $20; preceding bequests, to-
gether with prior gifts makes equal distribution.
    Teste., Phillip F. Pinnell, Benjamin Bassell, Goodman
Reger.
    Bk. A, pp. 172-174.   /110/

    SMALLRIDGE, WILLIAM, Upshur County, W. Va., 30 Mar.
1874; Apr. term, 1876.
    Wife CHARLOTTE, sons WILLIAM B., SAMUEL D., and JACOB J.
SMALLRIDGE, daus. MARY ELIZABETH CRITES, NANCY JANE DOUGLAS,
and MARGARET PHIPPS, heirs of PRISCILLA SMITH, deceased. No
ex. named.
    Testator bequeaths to wife CHARLOTTE SMALLRIDGE, $250,
also all household and kitchen furniture, also "the west end"
of the home during her life, also maintenance from son William
B. Smallridge; to son JACOB J. SMALLRIDGE, $500 to consist of
3 bonds given to testator, William B., and Samuel D. Smallridge
by sd. Jacob J., and sufficient livestock to complete bequast;
to dau. MARY ELIZABETH CRITES, livestock valued at $350; to
dau. NANCY JANE DOUGLAS, 2 bonds executed by Henry M. Douglas
and sufficient livestock to make total bequest of $250; to
dau. MARGARET PHIPPS, $250 to include 3 bonds executed by
George Phipps; to 3 heirs of testator's deceased dau. PRISCILLA
SMITH, $33.33 1/3 each; to sons WILLIAM and SAMUEL D. SMALLRIDGE,
equal division of realty and remaining personalty, sd. William
to provide for parents.
    Teste., Festus Young, Beecher W. Phillips.
    Bk. A, pp. 175, 176.   /111/

    DEEN, JOHN, Upshur County, W. Va., 15 Dec. 1875; 1 May
1876.
    Wife CATHARINE, sons JACOB, NICHOLAS, WILLIAM, MARSHALL,
GEORGE W., SOLOMON, JOHN, PERRY, and ELIAS DEEN, daus. JULIA
A. ROHRBOUGH, POLLY HUFFMAN, MALINDA SHEETS, ELIZABETH CRITES,
and LOUISA J. KESLING, heirs of dau. MATILDA HINKLE, grandson
JOHN B. DEEN, grdau. SALINA GOODEN. Solomon Deen, ex.
    Testator desires pmt. of debts and funeral expenses; be-
queaths to son JACOB DEEN, home farm of 108 a. and its appurtenances with provision that he care for testator's wife CATHARINE
DEEN, during her life; to sd. CATHARINE DEEN, in addition to
preceding provision, a bed and bedding; to son NICHOLAS, $50;
to son WILLIAM, $50; to son MARSHALL, $50; to son GEORGE W.,
$50; to son SOLOMON, $50; to son JOHN, $50; to son PERRY, $50;
to son ELIAS, $50; loans made by testator to children are to be

(112, 113)

pd. to estate and as follows: Marshall, $125, George W., $110, William, $35, Nicholas, $25, Perry, $50, John, $25, Julia A. Rohrbough, $25, Louisa J. Kesling, $25; to daus. JULIA A. ROHRBOUGH, POLLY HUFFMAN, MALINDA SHEETS, ELIZABETH CRITES, and LOUISA J. KESLING, $25 each; to children of testator's deceased dau. MATILDA HINKLE, $25 to be divided equally; to grandson JOHN B. DEEN, prior gift of horse, saddle, and bridle; to grdau. SALINA GOODEN, prior gift of 1 cow; personalty except that bequeathed to sd. Catharine to be sold and proceeds thereof divided among children and their heirs, each dau. and her heirs to receive ¼ less than each son and his heirs.
 Teste., John G. Dix, A. M. Poundstone.
 Bk. A, pp. 178-180.
 Renunciation. 26 Sept. 1876.
 CATHARINE DEEN renounces will of JOHN DEEN and provisions thereof, claiming her dower right in sd. estate.
 Bk. A, p. 182.
 Teste., J. T. Mayo.   /112/

 ESKEW, HENDLEY L., aged 87, Upshur County, W. Va., 25 Mar. 1874; 14 Aug. 1876.
 Wife CATHARINE, step-dau. SARAH FRANCES FLETCHER FOSTER, JOHN ESKEW, JAMES ESKEW, WILLIAM ESKEW, MARY ESKEW BOSTIC, LEWIS ANDERSON ESKEW, ELLIS ESKEW, GEORGE W. ESKEW, LLOYD ESKEW, FLOYD P. ESKEW, LORETTA JANE ESKEW (no relationship shown). Samuel Reese, ex.
 Testator desires pmt. of debts and that "funeral to be conducted in a befitting manner and body to be interred in the burying ground near residence of testator"; bequeaths to wife CATHARINE ESKEW, all realty and personalty for widowhood, in case of her remarriage or death, ex. to sell all realty and personalty and to make distribution of proceeds thereof as follows: to JOHN ESKEW, $20; to JAMES ESKEW, $20; to WILLIAM ESKEW, $20; to MARY ESKEW BOSTIC, $20; to LEWIS ANDERSON ESKEW, $20; to ELLIS ESKEW, prior gift of $20; to step-dau. SARAH FRANCES FLETCHER FOSTER, $20; remainder of estate to be equally divided among GEORGE W. ESKEW, LLOYD ESKEW, FLOYD P. ESKEW, and LORETTA JANE ESKEW, in case of death of all or any of last four named legatees, share or shares to descend equally to survivors.
 Teste., Watson Westfall, David Reese, E. C. Rollins.
 Bk. A, pp. 180-182.   /113/

 GRUBB, AMOS, Upshur County, W. Va., 21 Aug. 1876; 9 Oct. 1876.
 Dau. EMALINE WILFONG, grdau. MARIE ROBINSON.   No ex. named.
 Testator desires pmt. of debts and funeral expenses; bequeaths to dau. EMALINE WILFONG and her heirs, all realty and personalty; to grdau. MARIE ROBINSON, "a certain quilt"; no bequests to sons Thomas, Enoch and Andrew Grubb, daus. Mary

Ann Grubb, Sarah Reese, and Elizabeth Maxon, nor to son-in-law Thomas Robinson "as they have already received their share."
    Teste., Samuel Reese, George Warner, William N. Foster (his mark).
    Bk. A, p. 183.   /114/

    BENNETT, ISAIAH M., Upshur County, W. Va., 2 Sept. 1876; Oct. term, 1876.
    Wife MARY E., son CHARLES J. C. BENNETT, bros. SILAS W., and O. E. BENNETT. O. E. Bennett, ex.
    Testator desires pmt. of debts and funeral expenses; within 2 years after death of testator all realty and personalty to be sold; to wife MARY E. BENNETT, interest on 1/3 of proceeds from sd. sale, also $500; to son CHARLES J. C. BENNETT, interest on remainder of proceeds of sd. sale, principal to be used for his education if guardian so desires; when sd. Charles J. C. reaches legal age, he is to receive 1/3 of principal, the remainder to be pd. in equal installments when he reaches 22 and 23 yrs.; in case sd. Charles J. C. die without issue, then estate equally to bros. SILAS W. and O. E. BENNETT or survivor if one of them be dead; if both are dead then estate to their heirs; upon death of sd. Mary E. Bennett, her estate to sd. CHARLES J. C. in pmts. as provided in his bequest or if sd. Charles J. C. be dead, then her estate to Silas W. and O. E. Bennett as before provided.
    Teste., W. C. Carper, C. F. Ridgeway, C. C. Higginbotham.
    Bk. A, pp. 184-186.   /115/

    HERNDON, GEORGE T., Upshur County, W. Va., 11 Mar. 1873; 21 Nov. 1876.
    Wife MALINDA, CLAUDIUS B. MAYO (no relationship shown). Claudius B. Mayo, ex.
    Testator bequeaths to CLAUDIUS B. MAYO, $100; to wife MALINDA HERNDON, all remaining personalty and all realty.
    Teste., A. M. Poundstone, David S. Pinnell.
    Bk. A, p. 187.   /116/

    MORGAN, HATTIE, Edwards County, Ill., n.d.; Upshur County, W. Va., 7 Feb. 1877.
    MARY ANN MORGAN, OLIVE MORMAN, JANE MORGAN, ELIZABETH MORGAN, MARIA L. HART, LUCEBA MORGAN, GRACE H. MORGAN (no relationship shown). Eliza Rude, ex.
    Testatrix desires pmt. of debts and funeral expenses; bequeaths to MARY ANN MORGAN, OLIVE MORMAN, JANE MORGAN, ELIZABETH MORGAN, and MARIA L. HART, $25 each; to LUCEBA MORGAN, all remaining personalty and testatrix's "share of real estate at Bone Gap" with provision that she "will always provide for" GRACE H. MORGAN.
    Teste., Henry L. Dickson, Edwin F. Dickson.
    Bk. A, pp. 189, 190.   /117/

ABSTRACTS OF WILLS, 1851-1884

(118-120)

MORGAN, LYDIA N. /H.?/, Albon, Edwards County, Ill., 22 Jan. 1871; Upshur County, W. Va., 7 Feb. 1877.
MAXWELL W. MORGAN, heirs of AMOS B. MORGAN, ELIZABETH MORGAN, MILTON W. MORGAN, MARIA L. HART, LUCEBA MORGAN, and HATTIE MORGAN (no relationship shown). Hattie Morgan, ex.
Testatrix desires pmt. of debts and funeral expenses; if value of property be more than $2,000, then testatrix bequeaths to MAXWELL W. MORGAN, $200; to heirs of AMOS B. MORGAN, $50 each when they reach legal age with exception of ELIZABETH MORGAN and MILTON W. MORGAN, who are to receive their shares 1 year after probate of will; to MARIA L. HART, $300; to LUCEBA MORGAN, $50; any remaining personalty or realty to be equally divided among sd. LUCEBA, HATTIE, and GRACE H. MORGAN, if sd. Grace should die before reaching legal age, her share to be equally divided between sd. Luceba and Hattie.
Teste., Eliza Rude, Luceba Morgan.
Bk. A, pp. 188, 189.   /118/

MICK, MARY, Upshur County, W. Va., 5 July 1876; 17 Feb. 1877.
Sons NICHOLAS and ADAM MICK, dau. LUCINDA REXROAD. No ex. named.
Testatrix desires pmt. of debts and funeral expenses; also that grave stones be erected for herself, her deceased husband, and deceased son Elbridge, cost of sd. stones not to exceed more than $40; bequeaths to son NICHOLAS MICK, $\frac{1}{4}$ of remaining estate; to son ADAM MICK, 3/8 of estate; to dau. LUCINDA REXROAD, 3/8 of estate; also to sd. ADAM MICK a "certain lien" amounting to $112.50 "which testatrix lifted of Isaiah M. Bennett."
Teste., O. B. Loudin, G. J. Reeder.
Bk. A, pp. 190, 191.   /119/

BUCKANAN, ABRAM, Upshur County, W. Va., 26 June 1876; 16 Apr. 1877.
Sons JOHN W., and THOMAS BUCKANAN, dau.-in-law CAROLINE BUCKANAN, grandchildren MARTHA L. and HANSON B. BUCKANAN. No ex. named.
Testator bequeaths to son JOHN W. BUCKANAN, house, gun, large steel trap, and tools; to son THOMAS BUCKANAN, 1 feather bed and 1 coverlet; to dau-in-law CAROLINE, wife of Andrew C. BUCKANAN, remainder of household and kitchen furniture; to grandchildren MARTHA L., and HANSON B., children of Erskine BUCKANAN, deceased, $1 each.
Teste., Festus Young, Nancy Young (her mark).
Bk. A, p. 192.   /120/

WARD, JOSEPH, Upshur County, W. Va., 18 May 1877; 18 June 1877.
Wife REBECCA, bros. JOB and JACKSON WARD. Dr. P. F. Pinnell, ex.
Testator desires to be "decently buried in graveyard near Solomon Leonard"; also desires pmt. of debts and funeral

expenses from personalty; bequeaths to wife REBECCA WARD, all realty in town of Buckhannon, all household and kitchen furniture and remainder of personalty; upon death of sd. Rebecca, property to be equally divided between testator's bros. JOB and JACKSON WARD; to bro. JOB WARD, $200 in addition to prior bequest.

Teste., Jacob Waugh, P. F. Pinnell, J. M. Pinnell.
Bk. A, pp. 193, 194.
Renunciation. 6 May 1878.
REBECCA WARD, widow of JOSEPH WARD renounces provisions made for her in the will of her deceased husband.
Bk. A, p. 197. /121/

GREENE, WILLIAM, Upshur County, W. Va., n.d.; 17 Aug. 1877.
Wife MARY K., JEREMY GREENE, WILLIAM H. GREENE, MARY ANNE GREENE, BRIDGET GREENE, JOSEPH GREENE, JANE YOUNG, LESLIE LEMONS, ALVA LEMONS (no relationship shown). Mary K. Greene, ex.
Testator bequeaths to wife MARY K. GREENE, all personalty and realty; upon death of sd. Mary K. Greene, realty to JEREMY GREENE; to WILLIAM H. GREENE, 1 horse; to MARY ANNE GREENE, $100 and 1 cow; to BRIDGET GREENE, $20; to JOSEPH GREENE, $20; to JANE YOUNG, $20; to LESLIE and ALVA LEMONS, $10 each when they reach legal age; equal division of household and kitchen furniture among surviving heirs upon death of sd. Mary K. Greene.
Proven by: James Ludridge, Moses M. McCue, John J. Greene.
Bk. A, pp. 195, 196. /122/

FALLON, JOHN SR., Upshur County, W. Va., 14 June 1877; 18 Aug. 1877.
Son JOHN FALLON JR., dau. BESSIE FARLEY, other children not named. No ex. named.
Testator bequeaths to son JOHN FALLON JR., $250 in notes; to dau. BESSIE FARLEY, $10.25; to each of children (not named), 25¢.
Teste., Edward Gormley, Michael Fitzpatrick.
Bk. A, p. 196. /123/

LEWIS, MARY, Upshur County, W. Va., 21 Nov. 1878; 14 Dec. 1878.
Sons MARSHALL and JOHN LEWIS, daus. ELIZABETH HESS, and BALINDA HINKLE, grdaus. MARY FRANCIS LEWIS, LOUISA ELLEN LEWIS, children of James and John Lewis. No ex. named.
Testatrix desires that she be buried beside her husband John Lewis; bequeaths to son MARSHALL LEWIS, household and kitchen furniture, cooking utensils, cupboard and contents, 1 bureau, straw tick, 2 beds and bedsteads, 1 feather tick and feathers, 4 pillows, 2 bolsters, 2 sheets, 2 blankets, 2 coverlets, 2 comforts, share in other bedding, all table cloths,

1 cow, testatrix's saddle, a tin trunk "to be used for keep-
ing papers," ½ interest in dye kettle, and remainder of estate
after settlement; to son JOHN LEWIS, 1 large pot, ½ interest
in dye kettle, 1 bed and bedding, ½ of bedding remaining after
bequests are fulfilled; to grdau. MARY FRANCIS, dau. of James
LEWIS, 1 coverlet, 1 blanket, and 1 "long box"; to grdau.
LOUISA ELLEN LEWIS, 1 coverlet and 1 blanket; to dau. ELIZABETH
HESS, 2 flannel dresses, 1 red underskirt, all flannel capes,
all other capes, black silk bonnet, caps, black calico dress
with apron and cape; to dau. BALINDA HINKLE, 2 flannel dresses;
to children of sons James and John Lewis, remainder of clothing.
Teste., Jacob Waugh, Abram Post.
Bk. A, pp. 197, 198.   /124/

SIRON, VALENTINE, Upshur County, W. Va., 26 Dec. 1878; 10
Feb. 1879.
Sons JOSEPH, JOHN B., HENRY F., VALENTINE B., and WILLIAM
W. SIRON, daus. HANNAH M. SHOBE, MAGDALENE E., and LYDIA S.
SIRON. Son Valentine B. Siron, ex.
Testator desires pmt. of debts; bequeaths to son JOSEPH
SIRON, $1; to son JOHN B. SIRON, $1; to son HENRY F. SIRON, $1;
to dau. HANNAH M. SHOBE, $5; to dau. MAGDALENE E. SIRON, $50;
to dau. LYDIA S. SIRON, $50; to sd. daus. MAGDALENE and LYDIA,
living at home from proceeds of estate until they marry; to
sons VALENTINE B. SIRON and WILLIAM W. SIRON, remainder of
realty and personalty.
Teste., Adam P. Rusmissell, William N. Childress, Joseph
Crawford.
Bk. A, p. 199.   /125/

PRINGLE, JOEL, Upshur County, W. Va., 7 Jan. 1879; 8 Mar.
1879.
Wife ELIZA PRINGLE. No ex. named.
Testator desires pmt. of funeral expenses from personalty;
bequeaths to wife ELIZA, all personalty and realty consisting
of a house and lot on the east side of the Buckhannon and
Kanawha Turnpike joining lands of J. Hosaflook, William L.
Colerider and others, all household and kitchen furniture, and
1 cow.
Teste., S. J. Rohrbough, Daniel Cutright.
Bk. A, p. 200.   /126/

NEFF, JACOB, Upshur County, W. Va., 16 Nov. 1878; 15 Apr.
1879.
Wife, MARY A. NEFF, children MARY CATHARINE RIVES, BARBARA
ANN HEAVNER, ELIZABETH POTTER, and THOMAS H. NEFF, step-son
ROBERT TOMEY. Wife Mary A. Neff, ex.
Testator desires pmt. of debts and funeral expenses from
personalty; bequeaths to children MARY CATHARINE RIVES, BARBARA
ANN HEAVNER, ELIZABETH POTTER, and THOMAS A. NEFF, each 1 calf

or $8; to wife MARY, all personalty and realty to use "as she sees fit"; to step-son ROBERT TOMEY, 1 2-yr. old sorrel horse.
Teste., John B. Henderson, Asa Strader, John A. Hess.
Bk. A, pp. 201, 202. /127/

PERRY, HUBBARD B., Upshur County, W. Va., 6 Oct. 1877; 2 July 1879.
Wife HARRIET PERRY, daus. EMILINE E. and LUCY J. PERRY Lynn Phillips, ex.
Testator bequeaths to dau. EMILINE E. /PERRY/, 1 "speckled hen," 1 cow and calf, and share after death of testator's wife Harriet in estate; to dau. LUCY J. PERRY, 1 heifer and share in estate; to wife HARRIET, remainder of estate after pmt. of debts and bequests for life, upon her death sd. estate to be equally divided among living heirs (not named).
Teste., C. S. Haynes, M. A. Darnall, Lynn Phillips.
Bk. A, p. 203. /128/

McDOWELL, JOHN, Upshur County, W. Va., 2 Jan. 1879; 13 Oct. 1879.
Wife ANNA McDOWELL, son J. A. McDOWELL, dau. JANE DARNELL, W. E. McDOWELL (relationship not shown). J. M. Curry and R. A. Herring, exs.
Testator bequeaths to wife ANNA, 1 mare which upon sd. Anna's death is to be sold and the proceeds used to purchase stones for the graves of testator and sd. Anna, also to sd. ANNA, testator's beds and bedding "to dispose of at her pleasure"; to son J. A. McDOWELL, 1 colt, providing he pay sd. Anna a part of price of sd. colt "if necessary," also bookcase and books, and carpenter's tools; to W. E. McDOWELL (no relationship shown), proceeds of sale of testator's watch; to dau. JANE DARNELL, testator's bureau.
Teste., John N. Curry, Richard A. Herring.
Bk. A, p. 205. /129/

BOGGESS, JOHN L., Upshur County, W. Va., 22 Mar. 1879; 16 Oct. 1879.
Wife DELILA BOGGESS, sons HAYMOND and THOMAS BOGGESS, daus. MARY E. BENNETT, CELIA STANSBERRY, and NANCY BEER. Son Haymond Boggess, ex.
Testator desires pmt. of debts; bequeaths to wife DELILA, life use of all realty and personalty; upon death of sd. Delila, all estate to son HAYMOND BOGGESS with provision that he pay testator's dau. MARY E. BENNETT, $100; to children CELIA, wife of Elijah STANSBERRY, NANCY, wife of Reuben D. BEER, and THOMAS BOGGESS, prior gifts.
Teste., Jasper N. Westfall, George W. Starn.
Bk. A, p. 204. /130/

(131-133)

CURRY, ROBERT, Upshur County, W. Va., 28 Aug. 1879; 8 Nov. 1879.
Wife MARY J. CURRY, daus. VIRGINIA SMITH, MARY E. SMITH, and HATTIE A. CURRY, sons I. W., A. B., and ROBERT E. CURRY. Edward E. Curry, ex.
Testator desires pmt. of debts; bequeaths to dau. VIRGINIA SMITH, $1 and prior gift of $400; to son I. W. CURRY, $1 and prior gift of $400; to son A. B. CURRY, $1 and prior gift of $400; to dau. MARY E. SMITH, $1 and prior gift of $400; remain- of estate to be equally divided among wife MARY J. CURRY, dau. HATTIE A. CURRY, and son ROBERT E. CURRY.
Teste., I. W. Vincent, J. W. Windell.
Bk. A, pp. 207, 208.   /131/

ROHRBOUGH, RACHAEL E., Upshur County, W. Va., 8 Nov. 1879; 9 Jan. 1880.
Husband JOHN W. ROHRBOUGH, sons TROY M., and GUY E. ROHR- BOUGH. Husband John W. Rohrbough, ex.
Testatrix bequeaths to husband JOHN W. ROHRBOUGH, all per- sonalty; to sons TROY M., and GUY E. ROHRBOUGH, equal shares in the proceeds of sale of testatrix's realty in town of Grafton, Taylor County, W. Va., when they reach legal age, sd. property to be sold at death of testatrix and ex. to place pro- ceeds on interest using part of principal, if needed, for main- tenance and education of sd. Troy M. and Guy E.; if either of sd. heirs die before final distribution of sd. bequest, then property to remaining heir; if both die then property to sd. John W. Rohrbough.
Teste., W. C. Carper, S. S. Leonard, Levi Leonard.
Bk. A, pp. 209, 210.   /132/

LORENTZ, MARSHALL F., Upshur County, W. Va., 2 Sept. 1878; 7 May 1880.
Wife CARRIE E. LORENTZ, children IRA /IVA?/ J., MARAETTA A., and MARSHALL F. D. LORENTZ. Wife Carrie E. Lorentz, ex.
Testator desires to be buried "in graveyard near Solomon Leonards," also desires pmt. of debts and funeral expenses from personalty; bequeaths to wife CARRIE E. LORENTZ, all per- sonalty and realty for life or widowhood; upon death or re- marriage of sd. Carrie E., property to be equally divided among children IRA /IVA?/ J., MARAETTA A., and MARSHALL F. D. LORENTZ.
Teste., N. G. Mundy, James L. Smith, A. M. Poundstone.
Bk. A, pp. 211-213.   /133/

POST, DANIEL, Upshur County, W. Va., 7 July 1880; 21 July 1880.
Wife /MARY POST/, grdau. JANE POST, other heirs not named. Son Nicholas Post, ex.
Testator desires pmt. of debts and funeral expenses from public sale of personalty; bequeaths remainder of proceeds of sd. sale to be equally divided among lawful heirs (not named);

(134-136)

to grdau. JANE POST, her share of estate, 1 mare and "her
choice of the cows"; to wife /MARY POST7 "with whom I have
lived for sixty years" legal share in estate.
    Teste., Allen Lewis, J. N. McPherson, John W. McPherson.
    Bk. A, pp. 214, 215.
    Renunciation. 2 Oct. 1880.
    MARY POST, widow renounces will of DANIEL POST.
    Ackn. Silas Bennett, N.P.
    Bk. A, p. 215   /134_7

    McDERMOTT, JAMES SR., Upshur County, W. Va., 15 June
1880; 9 Aug. 1880.
    Wife not named, heirs of THOMAS McDERMOTT, LEWIS COOL,
JOHN McDERMOTT, PATRICK McDERMOTT, JAMES McDERMOTT JR.,
BRIDGET FLANAGAN, ANN CUNNINGHAM, (no relationship shown),
God-child FRANCIS McDERMOTT, bro. JOHN McDERMOTT. No ex.
named.
    Testator desires pmt. of funeral expenses; bequeaths to
wife (not named) all personalty except bequests for life use;
to heirs of THOMAS McDERMOTT, $1 and prior gifts to sd. Thomas;
to LEWIS COOL, $1; to JOHN McDERMOTT, $1 and prior gifts; to
PATRICK McDERMOTT, $1 and prior gifts; to JAMES McDERMOTT JR.,
$1 and prior gifts; to BRIDGET FLANAGAN, $50 and prior gifts;
to ANN CUNNINGHAM, $50 and prior gifts; to Godchild FRANCIS,
son of Patrick McDERMOTT, 1 horse, 1 duck, 10 sheep to be
sold upon death of testator, proceeds to bro. John McDermott
who is to be guardian and who is to invest money at interest
until sd. Patrick reaches age of 18; a note held by testator
against James McDermott Jr., to be applied toward bequest to
sd. Bridget Flanagan and Ann Cunningham.
    Teste., Valentine Hinkle Jr., Eli Painter.
    Bk. A, p. 216, 217.   /135_7

    HOLLEN, WELLINGTON, Upshur County, W. Va., 22 May 1880;
26 Feb. 1881.
    Wife ELIZABETH HOLLEN, sons WILLIAM F., JOHN A. and ZEBB
D. HOLLEN, daus. MARY ELIZABETH HOLLEN and one not named,
ALBERT G. REGER (relationship not shown). Martin M. Rice, ex.
    Testator desires pmt. of debts and funeral expenses; be-
queaths to wife ELIZABETH HOLLEN, home in town of Centerville,
also 42 a. adjoining, also wagon, harness, farming equipment,
household and kitchen furniture, grain, all moneys and bonds,
all accounts due testator, riding horse, cattle, hogs, watch,
millwright tools, books and papers; sd. Elizabeth is to care
for her widowed dau. (not named) as "long as she is able"; to
ALBERT G. REGER (no relationship shown), 1 horse; to son
WILLIAM F. HOLLEN, $1; to son JOHN A. HOLLEN, $1; to son ZEBB
D. HOLLEN, $1; to dau. MARY ELIZABETH HOLLEN, $1.
    Teste., Uriah Hevener, Samuel B. Hannah.
    Bk. A, pp. 218, 219.   /136_7

(137-139)

WILSON, SAMUEL, Upshur County, W. Va., 10 Mar. 1876; 25 Mar. 1881.
Wife ESTHER S. WILSON, sons JONATHAN and EVERETT S. WILSON, grandsons VERNON L. BENNETT, CLARENCE S. BENNETT, also EMILY GOLDEN, LUCETTA CURRY, LYDIA Y. VINCENT, and REBECCA L. ANDERSON. Lorenzo D. Anderson, ex.
Testator bequeaths to son JONATHAN WILSON, $1,000; to grandson VERNON L. BENNETT, son of Jemima S. Bennett, $100; to grandson CLARENCE S. BENNETT, son of sd. Jemima S., $100; to wife ESTHER S. WILSON and son EVERETT S. WILSON jointly, 147 a. "lying on the left hand side of the road" with provision that sd. Esther S. and Everett S. to pay $600 for sd. land in 5 years after testator's death; in case sd. Everett S. should die before reaching legal age, sd. Esther S. to have one half of sd. land including house, other half to be equally divided among all heirs of testator; all remaining personalty to EMILY GOLDEN, LUCETTA CURRY, LYDIA Y. VINCENT, and REBECCA L. ANDERSON (no relationship shown).
Teste., James A. Strader, John M. Armstrong.
Bk. A, pp. 220, 221.   /137/

CLARK, JANE, Buckhannon, Upshur County, W. Va., 31 Dec. 1880; 9 May 1881.
Dau. MAY BASTABLE, son MILTON BASTABLE. Dau. May Bastable, ex.
Testatrix desires pmt. of debts and funeral expenses; bequeaths all realty and personalty to dau. MAY BASTABLE and son MILTON BASTABLE, sd. estate to remain intact until sd. Milton reaches legal age; ½ of interest arising from personalty to be used for maintenance, education, and benefit of sd. Milton; when sd. Milton reaches age of 21 all realty to be sold and equal distribution made.
Teste., John Mullins, Virginia Mullins, W. G. L. Totten.
Bk. A, pp. 221-223.   /138/

BARGERHOFF, JONAS, Upshur County, W. Va., 6 June 1881; 5 July 1881.
Wife LETICCIA BARGERHOFF, dau-in-law MARGARET BARGERHOFF and children. Son Abner Bargerhoff, ex.
Testator desires pmt. of debts and funeral expenses from personalty; bequeaths to wife LETICCIA BARGERHOFF, for life or widowhood, all realty and personalty; upon death or remarriage of sd. Leticcia, property to dau-in-law MARGARET, wife of son Abner BARGERHOFF and heirs.
Teste., T. M. Allman, Clara P. Bargerhoff, Sallie Bargerhoff, Jacob Waugh.
Bk. A, p. 224.   /139/

CUTRIGHT, LOT, farmer, Upshur County, W. Va., 16 May 1881; 26 Aug. 1881.
Wife ISABEL CUTRIGHT, daus. VICTORIA CUTRIGHT, NAOMI ROLLINS, ADALINE FARRAR, and ALICE I. JACK, grandchildren

(140-142)

MARGARET S. CRISLIP, ISAAC M. HINKLE, E. D. HINKLE, MARY J. HINKLE, H. M. HINKLE, MINNIE F. HINKLE, LAVINA TEETS, NAOMI TEETS, and MARGARET TEETS. Ishmael Cutright of Hinkleville, ex.

Testator desires pmt. of debts and funeral expenses from personalty; bequeaths to grandchildren, MARGARET S. CRISLIP, ISAAC M. HINKLE, E. D. HINKLE, MARY J. HINKLE, H. M. HINKLE, and MINNIE F. HINKLE, heirs of testator's deceased dau. Clarissa Hinkle, $20 each when they arrive at legal age and prior gift to sd. Clarissa of $150; to dau. VICTORIA CUTRIGHT, prior gift of land valued at $450; to dau. NAOMI ROLLINS, prior gift of land valued at $440; to dau. ADALINE FARRAR, prior gift of land valued at $440; to grandchildren LAVINA TEETS, NAOMI TEETS, and MARGARET TEETS, heirs of testator's deceased dau. Ethelinda Teets, prior gift of /land/ valued at $440; to dau. ALICE I. JACK, prior gift of land valued at $440; to wife ISABEL CUTRIGHT, remainder of all realty and personalty.
Teste., S. J. Rohrbough, Abram Strader.
Bk. A, pp. 226, 227.   /140/

CONLEY, BENJAMIN, Upshur County, W. Va., 20 Aug. 1878; 27 Aug. 1881.
Wife LYDDA CONLEY, children not named. No ex. named.
Testator desires pmt. of debts and funeral expenses; bequeaths to wife LYDDA CONLEY, all realty and personalty for life to be used for supporting children with provision that 15 a. of realty lying on the Westfall line may be sold by sd. Lydda; on death of sd. Lydda remaining property to be divided equally among "all children."
Teste., O. B. Loudin, L. W. Loudin, N. W. Loudin.
Bk. A, pp. 225.   /141/

HINKLE, ABRAHAM, Upshur County, W. Va., n.d.; 8 Nov. 1881.
Wife MARY ANN HINKLE, son JONAS B. HINKLE, sons-in-law, ISHMAEL CUTRIGHT and GRANVILLE S. CUTRIGHT, 2 grandchildren not named. Ex. not named.
Testator desires pmt. of debts and funeral expenses; bequeaths to wife MARY ANN HINKLE, 1 horse, 1 cow, all farming implements, household and kitchen furniture, and all crops for life or widowhood; to two grandchildren (not named), sons of H. J. Hinkle, $470 to be paid "severally" when they reach age of 21; to son JONAS B. HINKLE, 60 a. of land on Middle Fork /River/ waters; to sons-in-law ISHMAEL CUTRIGHT and GRANVILLE S. CUTRIGHT, prior gifts of land.
Teste., Simeon J. Rohrbough, Asby P. Cutright.
Bk. A, pp. 228, 229.
Renunciation. 13 Dec. 1881.
MARY ANN HINKLE renounces provisions of will of husband ABRAHAM HINKLE.
Ackn., Daniel Cutright. N.P.
Bk. A, p. 229.   /142/

(143,144)

WARD, JACKSON, Upshur County, W. Va., 18 Jan. 1882; 30
Mar. 1882.
Wife VASHTI WARD, son JOHN W. WARD. John A. Crislip, ex.
Testator desires pmt. of debts and funeral expenses from
realty; bequeaths to wife VASHTI, all household and kitchen
furniture, and all personalty other than that included in firm;
desires that as soon as possible an inventory be made of stock
of mercantile business in which testator and son John W. are
engaged and that sd. John W. execute a bond to sd. Vashti for
her share in the firm.
Teste., S. G. Kesling, A. S. Swick, O. E. Bennett.
Bk. A, pp. 230, 231.   /143/

CARPER, BENJAMIN, Upshur County, W. Va., 25 Feb. 1881; 3
May 1882.
Wife ANNA CARPER, dau. CARIE C. CARPER. Wife Anna Carper,
ex.
Testator desires pmt. of debts and funeral expenses from
personalty; equal division of remainder of personalty and all
realty to wife ANNA and dau. CARIE C.; in case of death of
either legatee, survivor to become heir.
Teste., Levi Leonard, Silas Bennett, Jacob Waugh.
Bk. A, pp. 232, 233.   /144/

HAYWOOD, GEORGE, Mount Holly, Burlington County, N. J.,
7 Jan. 1875; Upshur County, W. Va., 19 June 1882.
Dau. SARAH MARIAN SHREVE, grandchildren BENJAMIN F. H.
SHREVE and MARIAN H. SHREVE. Friends Allen Fenimore and Harris
Cox, grandson Benjamin F. H. Shreve, exs.
Testator desires pmt. of debts and funeral expenses; bequeaths estate to exs. and their survivors for use of testator's dau. SARAH MARIAN SHREVE during her life and equal division for her children BENJAMIN F. H. SHREVE and MARIAN H.
SHREVE upon her death; exs. are to sell realty and collect
money, investing proceeds in bonds and mortgage on real estate,
interest accruing thereon to sd. SARAH MARIAN and at her death,
principal and interest equally to sd. BENJAMIN F. H. and MARIAN
H.; in case either sd. BENJAMIN F. H. or MARIAN H. die without
issue, then property to survivor; if litigation involving testator's land in French Creek, Upshur County, W. Va., not be
settled prior to probate of will, then exs. to carry on prose-
cution of suit and if sd. property is recovered, exs. to sell
same and give deeds therefor; proceeds of sd. sale, after pmt.
of costs, to sd. dau. SARAH MARIAN SHREVE; under no circum-
stances is son-in-law Benjamin F. Shreve to have any part of
estate and any moneys pd. to sd. SARAH MARIAN are to be in her
control.
Teste., Walter Ward, James N. Stratton.
Bk. A, pp. 233-244.
Codicil. 29 Jan. 1876.
Testator has, since making will, purchased large tract of
land in Webster and Nicholas Counties, W. Va., and has claims
in several other counties; places sd. property "in the same

(145-148)

position as directed in the will and subject to all the limit-
ations as set forth in sd. will and giving a devisee the same
accordingly."
Teste., James N. Stratton, Frank Scholfield.
Bk. A, p. 235. /145/

CURRY, MARY, Upshur County, W. Va., 26 June 1882; 5 July
1882.
Daus. SUSAN CURRY, LYDIA WILSON, SALLY ANN CAMPBELL,
LOUISA SPORE, sons JAMES, JOHN H., JAMES M., AND E. E. CURRY,
and NANCY VALENIA MEARNS (relationship not shown), grdau.
FLORENCE McWHORTER. G. H. Wilson, ex.
Testatrix desires pmt. of debts and funeral expenses, and
purchase of "plain marble tombstones"; bequeaths to dau. SUSAN
CURRY, 1 saddle; to dau. LYDIA WILSON, $10; to grdau. FLORENCE
McWHORTER, $4; to children of testatrix and Robert Curry, de-
ceased, as follows: JAMES CURRY, JOHN H. CURRY, SALLY ANN
CAMPBELL, LOUISA SPORE, JAMES MEARNS, and E. E. CURRY, $1 each;
to NANCY VALENIA MEARNS, remainder of estate for caring for
testatrix during the last 6 yrs. of her life.
Teste., James W. Windell, James H. Andrew, W. H. Curry.
Bk. A, p. 245. /146/

BEAN, HENRY, Upshur County, W. Va., 3 June 1880; 30 Aug.
1882.
Wife JULIA A. BEAN, sons HIRAM, JOHN WILLIAM, CHARLES,
NATHAN D., and GABRIEL BEAN, daus. SUSAN C. WAYTES, MARY J.
ALLMAN, HANNAH I. TENNEY, ANN M. CUTRIGHT, MILLY R. PHILLIPS,
and ELIZABETH BEAN. Wife Julia A. and son Nathan D. Bean,
exs.
Testator bequeaths $1 each to sons HIRAM, JOHN WILLIAM,
and CHARLES BEAN; $1 each to daus. SUSAN C. WAYTES, MARY J.
ALLMAN, HANNAH I. TENNEY, ANN M. CUTURIGHT, and MILLY R.
PHILLIPS; to dau. ELIZABETH M., ½ of home farm; to son NATHAN
D. BEAN, 40 a. "on which he now resides"; to son GABRIEL BEAN,
$100 less $25, the price of a cow; to wife JULIA A. BEAN, the
"mill property" and ½ of the home farm; to sd. JULIA A. and
ELIZABETH M., equal division of personalty, farm implements,
and household and kitchen furniture.
Teste., George E. Boseley, Joseph Huffman.
Bk. A, pp. 249, 250. /147/

SMITH, VIRGINIA, Upshur County, W. Va., 18 Sept. 1882;
2 Oct. 1882.
Husband WILLIAM SMITH. Ex. not named.
Testatrix desires pmt. of medical and funeral expenses;
bequeaths all realty and personalty to husband WILLIAM SMITH.
Teste., A. G. Musgrave, G. Austin Newlon, M. E. Shreve.
Bk. A, p. 251. /148/

(149-152)

WOODLEY, A. VIRGINIA, Upshur County, W. Va., 14 Jan. 1875; 6 Nov. 1882.
Husband WILLIS H. WOODLEY, son WILLIS H. WOODLEY JR., sister-in-law ELIZABETH H. H. WOODLEY. No ex. named.
Testatrix bequeaths all realty and personalty to son WILLIS H. WOODLEY JR., with provision that he care for testatrix' husband WILLIS H. WOODLEY and sister-in-law ELIZABETH H. H. WOODLEY during their lives.
Teste., Mifflin G. Gregory, E. E. H. Woodley, C. B. Mayo.
Bk. A, pp. 252, 253. /149/

MAYS, WILLIS, Upshur County, W. Va., 26 May 1877; 6 Jan. 1883.
Wife MANERVA MAYS. No ex. named.
Testator bequeaths to wife MANERVA, house, lot and all personalty.
Teste., Isaac Ours, Jacob F. Rohrbough.
Bk. B, pp. 58, 59. /150/

ASHWORTH, JAMES, Upshur County, W. Va., 28 Jan. 1882; 26 Mar. 1883.
Wife MARGARET ASHWORTH, children not named. Wife Margaret Ashworth, ex.
Testator bequeaths to wife MARGARET ASHWORTH all realty and personalty and "full control of any business"; sd. Margaret to have control of children and distribute property as she desires.
Teste., C. L. Denison, J. W. Hickman, S. H. Loudin (his mark).
Bk. A, pp. 247, 248. /151/

ROHRBOUGH, MARGARET, Upshur County, W. Va., 9 Jan. 1883; 26 Mar. 1883.
Husband M. L. ROHRBOUGH, mother CATHERINE McNULTY, sons IRVINE and WILLIAM ROHRBOUGH. Husband M. L. Rohrbough and son Irvine Rohrbough, exs.
Testatrix desires that home on the Island nr. Buckhannon which testatrix purchased from her father's estate be rented and from rent exs. to pay to her mother CATHERINE McNULTY, $120 annually for life; exs. may sell property and place $2,000 on interest, sd. interest to be pd. to sd. Catherine McNulty; husband M. L. ROHRBOUGH and sons IRVINE and WILLIAM may retain property with the provision that they pay sd. Catherine McNulty $120 annually for life; residue of estate or sale of property to be divided equally between sd. M. L. ROHRBOUGH, IRVINE ROHRBOUGH, and WILLIAM ROHRBOUGH; equal distribution of personalty as preceding bequest.
Teste., J. Leeroy Heavner, B. S. Dix, Jacob Waugh.
Bk. A, p. 253-255. /152/

WESTFALL, ELI W., Upshur County, W. Va., 5 Mar. 1883; 10 Apr. 1883.
Wife SAMANTHA WESTFALL. No ex. named.
Testator bequeaths all realty and personalty to wife SAMANTHA for widowhood or until youngest child reaches age of

(153-155)

16; if sd. Samantha remarry, or when youngest child reaches
16, realty and personalty to be divided as follows: to
SAMANTHA, her dower right, remainder to be equally divided
among children (not named).
    Teste., S. T. Westfall, David Reese, Zebedee Westfall.
    Bk. A, pp. 256, 257. /153/

    MARPLE, MARY R., Upshur County, W. Va., 9 Apr. 1883;
21 July 1883.
    Father ABRAM BENNETT. No ex. named.
    Testatrix bequeaths to father ABRAM BENNETT, 1 horse,
saddle, bridle, 2 beds and bedding, 3 quilts, 1 cooking stove
and utensils, 1 table, 1 set of chairs, 2 towels, 1 vegetable
dish, 1 meat dish, 1 molasses can, 1 bowl, 1 salt set, 1 pep-
per box, 1 set of knives and forks, 2 sets of spoons, 2 pie
plates, 1 cake stand, 1 set of glassware, 6 glass tumblers,
1 set of cups, saucers, and plates, 2 crocks, 2 table cloths,
1 window curtain, 1 glass pitcher, 1 bucket, 1 wash pan, 1
coffee mill, 1 smoothing iron, 1 safe, 23 yds. of carpet, also
title to all property belonging to testatrix with provision
that he care for testatrix until her death.
    Teste., O. B. Loudin, J. A. Teets.
    Bk. A, pp. 257, 288. /154/

    HINKLE, MARTIN, Upshur County, W. Va., 1 Jan. 1883; 21
Sept. 1883.
    Wife OLIVE HINKLE, mother-in-law, ELIZABETH KESLING.
Wife Olive Hinkle, ex.
    Testator desires pmt. of debts and funeral expenses; de-
sires completion of agreement between self and John W. Warner
regarding rental of farm, at death of mother-in-law, Elizabeth Kesling, and wife Olive Hinkle, property to sd. Warner as
by agreement, until sd. deaths, sd. Elizabeth Kesling and
Olive Hinkle to hold lien on property; bequeaths to sd.
ELIZABETH KESLING and OLIVE HINKLE, all rents and profits
from land leased to sd. Warner; to wife OLIVE, life interest
in 75 a. conveyed to testator by Middleton and Shreve, and
the residue of the home farm; upon death of sd. Olive, title
to foregoing bequest to be vested in IDA JANE WARNER, dau. of
afsd. John W. Warner; if sd. Ida Jane Warner die without issue
before sd. Olive Hinkle, then property to heirs of sd. Olive
Hinkle; to wife OLIVE HINKLE, all personalty and realty not
otherwise bequeathed, including house and lot in Buckhannon
and an undivided half in 55 a. deeded to Anthony Hinkle and
testator by Joel Foster.
    Teste., J. D. Adkison, S. Westfall.
    Bk. A, pp. 293-295. /155/

    CARPER, GEORGE, Upshur County, W. Va., 28 June 1876;
29 Sept. 1883.
    Wife RACHAEL CARPER, sons GEORGE COLUMBUS, DANIEL J.,
ISAAC, and ASA CARPER, daus. SARAH ELIZABETH REGER, MINERVA
McCARTY. Ebenezer Leonard, ex.

(156, 157)

Testator desires pmt. of debts and funeral expenses; bequeaths to wife RACHAEL CARPER all household furniture, bedding, carpets, all personalty, horses, farming utensils, money and rents on all lands held by testator and sd. Rachael; if sd. Rachael dies before testator, then sd. bequest to Rachael, to dau. SARAH ELIZABETH, wife of Montable REGER, and to son GEORGE COLUMBUS CARPER, to be divided as follows: to dau. Sarah Elizabeth, all household furniture and ½ of any money or bonds; to son George Columbus, remainder of personalty, ½ of money or bonds, and any rents due testator at his death from lands held by testator and sd. Rachael; if either of sd. heirs die before testator, then their shares to any children surviving.
Teste., John G. Dix, Jacob Waugh, Stark W. Arnold.
Bk. A, pp. 289-293.
Codicil. 28 June 1876.
Testator George Carper directs that if either dau. Sarah E. Reger or son George C. Carper die without issue, then property to be equally divided among heirs of surviving son or dau.
Teste., John G. Dix, Jacob Waugh, Stark W. Arnold.
Codicil. 25 Jan. 1879.
Testator George Carper adds codicil stating that only 2 of his children have been mentioned in will because others have received prior gifts making their share in estate. Names these sons and daus. as DANIEL J. CARPER, ISAAC CARPER, ASA CARPER, and MINERVA McCARTY.
Teste., John G. Dix, Stark W. Arnold.   /156/

ANDREWS, MORDICAI L., Upshur County, W. Va., 28 Apr. 1883; 16 Oct. 1883.
Wife SOPHIA ANDREWS, daus. LAUNA OLIVE ANDREWS, DELILA KUHN of McConnelsville, Ohio, MELISSA DAVIS of Ringold, Morgan County, Ohio, and BINY E. SNELL, of Morgan County, Ohio. No ex. named.
Testator desires pmt. of funeral expenses; also desires a "plain coffin and a plain marble slab lettered substantially"; bequeaths to wife SOPHIA ANDREWS, prior gift of a farm on Big Sand Run in Upshur County, also all livestock, farm equipment and household goods, she waiving further claim on estate; to dau. LAUNA OLIVE ANDREWS of Ohio, 1/3 of remainder of estate; to daus. DELILA KUHN of McConnelsville, Ohio, MELISSA DAVIS of Ringold, Morgan County, Ohio, and BINY E. SNELL of Morgan County, Ohio, equal division of remaining estate.
Teste., John A. Harris, Robert A. Manley.
Codicil. 15 June 1883.
Testator bequeaths to dau. LAUNA OLIVE ANDREWS, all household furniture, harness, work and saddlery, all claims, bonds, and mortgages on land, other heirs having received their share of estate.
Teste., John A. Harris, Robert A. Manley.
Bk. A, pp. 296, 297.   /157/

WARD, JOHN W., Upshur County, W. Va., 16 Jan. 1884; 18 Feb. 1884.
Wife, not named. John A. Crislip, ex.
Testator desires pmt. of debts and funeral expenses from sale of personalty; bequeaths to wife (not named), remainder of personalty and realty to be used for the maintenance and care of two infant children (not named).
Teste., John Karickhoff, S. G. Kesling, O. B. Loudin.
Bk. A, p. 298.   /158/

COLLINS, LEWIS, Upshur County, W. Va., 16 Feb. 1884; 8 Apr. 1884.
Heirs of dau., Mary Friend: ELIZABETH JORDAN, JAMES COLLINS, SARAH L. DAVIDSON, and LEWIS A. FRIEND; MARGARET J. COLLINS and CHARLES A. COLLINS (relationship not shown). No ex. named.
Testator bequeaths to heirs of dau. Mary Friend, ELIZA-BETH JORDAN, JAMES COLLINS, SARAH L. DAVIDSON, and LEWIS A. FRIEND, $1 each; to "lawful heirs" MARGARET J. COLLINS and CHARLES L. COLLINS, equal division of personalty and realty in Upshur County.
Teste., Wirt P. Conrad, Andrew J. McKessic, John M. Curry.
Bk. A, pp. 299, 300.   /159/

SHAVER, JOHN, farmer, French Creek, Upshur County, W. Va., 4 Mar. 1884; 29 Apr. 1884.
Wife RACHAEL SHAVER, grandson SAMUEL J. SANDERS, daus. ELIZABETH MILES and MARGARET SANDERS. Dr. J. J. Morgan of French Creek, ex.
Testator bequeaths to wife RACHAEL SHAVER, all realty and personalty for life; upon death of sd. Rachael property to be distributed as follows: to grandson SAMUEL J. SANDERS, all personalty and 60 a. being "that part of the home farm known as the Vance Tract," also 3 a. of that "part of the home farm known as the Sanders Tract, the coal privelege to be set off to the sd. Samuel J. Sanders"; to daus. ELIZABETH MILES and her heirs and MARGARET SANDERS and her heirs, equal division of remaining realty; Chapman McCoy and J. J. Morgan to act as commissioners in division of land.
Teste., Perry Tolbert, William J. Gibson.
Bk. A, pp. 300, 301.   /160/

BARTLETT, R/ANSDELL/, Upshur County, W. Va., 25 Dec. 1883; 2 June 1884.
Wife SUSANNA BARTLETT, daus. ELIZA A., REBECCA H., and ELIZABETH F. BARTLETT. No ex. named.
Testator bequeaths to wife SUSANNA BARTLETT, all realty and personalty for life or as long as she may wish to live on the farm; after death of sd. Susanna, realty to be equally divided among daus. ELIZA A., REBECCA H., and ELIZABETH F. BARTLETT or surviving heirs; personalty to be disposed of as sd. Susanna desires.
Teste., John G. Hoff, B. F. Moore.
Bk. A, p. 302.   /161/

(162, 163)

WARD, KINSEY, Upshur County, W. Va., 6 Apr. 1883; 2 July 1884.
Wife SOPHIA A. WARD, sons WILLIS O. B. WARD, JESSE C. WARD, MARTIN V. WARD, and NELSON R. WARD, daus. MELVINA HINKLE, MARTHA A. LANCE, BARBARA E. RENOLS, grandsons C. S. WARD, LETCHER WARD, and JOHN WARD. Son Willis O. B. Ward, Ephriam Snyder, Albert Zickefoose, exs.
Testator desires pmt. of debts and funeral expenses; bequeaths to sons WILLIS O. B. WARD and JESSE C. WARD, equal division of the home farm, farming utensils, all carpenter and joining instruments, horses, cattle, sheep, hogs, with the exception of 1 cow, all money in hand, and all notes due with the exception of one on James Wentz with provision that sd. sons "are to keep and maintain of the home farm as long as she remains a widow, wife SOPHIA S. WARD and see that she shall have the liberty of a bed and bedroom, the privilege and use of a riding beast, and a right to go and come as she pleases"; also to sd. SOPHIA S. WARD, 1 cow "whose productions shall be sold 6 months after birth"; to son MARTIN V. WARD, "remainder of borrowed money due testator"; to son NELSON R. WARD, $5; to MELVINA HINKLE, $5; to dau. MARTHA A. LANCE, $25; to dau. BARBARA E. RENOLS, $25; to grandsons C. S. WARD, LETCHER WARD, and JOHN WARD, $75 each; all bequests of money to be pd. from James Wentz note.
Teste., Ephram Snyder, Albert Zickefoose.
Bk. A, pp. 303, 304.   /162/

THRASH, H. J., Upshur County, W. Va., 13 June 1884; 8 July 1884.
Wife MELISSA J. THRASH, DAVID H. THRASH, MICHAEL THRASH (relationship not shown). George M. Blair, ex.
Testator bequeaths to DAVID H. THRASH, $500; to MICHAEL THRASH, $500; to wife MELISSA J. THRASH, remainder of property.
Teste., G. E. Post, Columbus McPherson, John S. Talbott.
Bk. A, p. 305.   /163/

WAUGH, JACOB, Buckhannon, Upshur County, W. Va., 16 Apr. 1884; 23 July 1884.
Wife MARGARETTA WAUGH, sons BROWN M., ENOCH L., JOHN W. W., and HOMER N. WAUGH, grdaus. MARY EMMA FULTZ FOSTER and PRUDY SMITH. Son Enoch L. Waugh, ex.
Testator bequeaths to wife MARGARETTA WAUGH, all household goods "which she brought with her at the time of her marriage," also money and bonds "which belong to her," also testator's silver watch for life; ex. is to sell at public sale 6 a. of land bought from T. G. Farnsworth, the proceeds to be used for pmt. of debts and any remaining to be equally divided among sons BROWN M., ENOCH L., JOHN W. W., and HOMER N. WAUGH; ex. is to sell house and lot #89 in Buckhannon and from proceeds thereof to pay to grdau. PRUDY SMITH, $100, remainder of proceeds of sale to grdau. MARY EMMA FULTZ FOSTER; upon death of

sd. Margaretta property to be distributed as follows: to
grdau. MARY EMMA FULTZ FOSTER, all bedding; to son BROWN M.
WAUGH,"large, six-legged table"; to son ENOCH H., first choice
of a table; to son JOHN W. W., second choice of a table; to
son HOMER N., third choice of a table; to grdau. MARY EMMA
FULTZ, wife of William A. FOSTER, fourth choice of a table;
to sons ENOCH L., and HOMER N., each 1 bookcase; to sd. MARY
EMMA FULTZ FOSTER, tin-doored safe; to grdau. PRUDY SMITH,
dau. of Leah Smith, deceased, family Bible and Hymn book; to
sons BROWN W., ENOCH L., HOMER N., and JOHN W. W., remainder
of books; remainder of property to be sold and equally divided among living children; after death of wife Margaretta,
silver watch to son HOMER N., or, if he be dead, to ENOCH L.
WAUGH.
> Teste., C. W. Hart, Allen A. Simpson, William C. Carper.
> Bk. A, pp. 307-309.
> Renunciation. 23 July 1884.
> MARGARETTA, widow of JACOB WAUGH, renounces provisions
of above will and claims dower right.
> Teste., none.
> Bk. A, p. 309.   /164/

BRYAN, JAMES, Upshur County, W. Va., 10 Jan. 1884; July
term, 1884.
> Son HENRY F. BRYAN, dau. MARTHA J. OURS, sons-in-law
DANIEL TENNEY, JOHN J. MOSS, grandsons DOW BRYAN, JAMES F.
OURS, grdau. MARY STRADER. Mearbeck Ours, ex.
> Testator desires pmt. of funeral expenses; bequeaths to
son HENRY F. BRYAN, $1 in addition to prior gift of $30; to
son-in-law DANIEL /DAVID ?/ TENNEY, $1 in addition to tomb-
stones for sd. Daniel's wife, valued at $25; to son-in-law
JOHN J. MOSS, $1 in addition to tombstones for sd. John's wife,
valued at $25; to grandson DOW BRYAN, $1; to grandson JAMES
F. OURS, $1; to grdau. MARY STRADER, $1; to dau. MARTHA J.,
wife of Mearbeck Ours, remainder of personalty and realty.
> Teste., Thomas A. Norvell, George Wilfong, Daniel Cutright.
> Bk. A, pp. 306, 307.   /165/

YOAKEM, JOHN, Upshur County, W. Va., 25 Aug. 1872; 26
Sept. 1884.
> Wife SARAH A. YOAKEM, sons EDWIN S. D., JAMES M., GEORGE
W., and NOAH YOAKEM, dau. JANE YOAKEM. Son Edwin S. D. Yoakem,
ex.
> Testator bequeaths to wife SARAH A. YOAKEM, life use of
livestock, farm equipment, household and kitchen furniture with
provision that son EDWIN S. D., have use of property and farm;
upon death of sd. Sarah A., property to be equally divided
among children JANE, JAMES M., and EDWIN S. D.; to sons GEORGE
W. and NOAH YOAKEM, prior gifts.
> Teste., C. B. Mayo, of Upshur County, and Thomas N. Bart-
lett (his mark) of Barbour County.
> Bk. A, p. 310.   /166/

(167, 168)

HEAVNER, ELIAS, Upshur County, W. Va., 14 Mar. 1883; 13 Oct. 1884.

Wife ELIZABETH HEAVNER, sons JACOB W., and CLARK W., dau. CATHERINE C. CARPER, grdaus. LENORA E. HEAVNER, ELLEN MAY FLEMING, and EMMA FLEMING CRAWFORD. Son Jacob W. Heavner, ex.

Testator desires pmt. of debts and funeral expenses; bequeaths to son JACOB W., $133.25 with interest from Mar. 12, 1883; after pmt. of debts and funeral expenses, remaining realty and personalty to be set aside for wife ELIZABETH HEAVNER, to be held in trust by ex.; upon death of sd. Elizabeth, executor to distribute estate as follows: to LENORA HEAVNER, dau. of testator's deceased son T. S. Heavner, $100; to JACOB W. HEAVNER, $300; to ELLEN MAY FLEMING, dau. of testator's deceased son, R. L. D. Heavner, $100; to EMMA CRAWFORD, sister of sd. Ellen May Fleming, $100; if estate is not sufficient to make sd. distribution, then distribution to be made in proportion; if any estate remain after distribution, then remainder to be equally divided in five equal parts: to son CLARK W. HEAVNER, dau. CATHERINE C. CARPER, sd. LENORA E. HEAVNER, sd. son JACOB W. HEAVNER, remaining 5th to sd. ELLEN MAY FLEMING and ELLEN CRAWFORD; to son CLARK W. HEAVNER and dau. CATHERINE C. CARPER, prior gifts.

Teste., Jacob Waugh, A. M. Poundstone.
Bk. A, p. 311-313.   /167/

RIFFLE, GEORGE E., Banks District, Upshur County, W. Va., 21 Nov. 1884; 8 Dec. 1884.

Wife DELILLY E. RIFFLE, JOHN R., and ULYSSES GRANT RIFFLE, DORA S., VICTORIA E., PENELLOPE, and MARY BELLE /RIFFLE ?/, ALBERT /RIFFLE ?/, and 6 children not named. Ex. ?

Testator desires pmt. of debts and funeral expenses from personalty; bequeaths to wife DELILLY E., $500 in place of dower; to "five children by first wife," $5; to JOHN R. RIFFLE (relationship not shown), all land on west or southwest end of testator's farm; to ULYSSES GRANT RIFFLE, (relationship not shown), when he reaches age of 21, all realty with provision that he pay to "his sisters" DORA S., VICTORIA E., PENELLOPE, and MARY BELLE, $50 each; to ALBERT (no relationship shown), "if he lives," support from proceeds of farm; "to the child just born" support from proceeds of farm; all remaining personalty after pmt. of debts to remain on farm.

Teste., S. Williams, Jonathan M. Riffle, John S. Riggleman.
Bk. A, p. 313, 314.
Renunciation. 6 Mar. 1885.
DELILA, widow of GEORGE E. RIFFLE, relinquishes bequest and desires dower right as if sd. George had died intestate.
Bk. A, p. 320.   \   /168/

NAME INDEX

(Numbers refer to entries)   (Abb-Bas)

Abbott, Daniel,
  will of, 5
Abbott, Frances,
  leg., 5
Abbott, John W.,
  leg., 5
Adkinson, J. D.,
  teste., 155
Allen, William,
  teste., 95
Allman, George,
  teste., 50
Allman, Mary J.,
  leg., 147
Allman, T. M.,
  teste., 139
Anderson, Lorenza D.,
  ex., 137
Anderson, Rebecca L.,
  leg., 137
Andrew, James H.,
  teste., 146
Andrews, Mordicai L.,
  will of, 157
Andrews, Olive,
  leg., 157
Andrews, Sophia,
  leg., 157
Armstrong, Elizabeth,
  heirs of, 71
Armstrong, Jared,
  line of, 24
Armstrong, John M.,
  teste., 137
Armstrong, Sarah,
  leg., 24
Arnold, Stark W.,
  teste., 156
Ashworth, James,
  will of, 151
Ashworth, Margaret,
  ex., 151
  leg., 151
Austin, G.,
  teste., 98

Balsley, George W.,
  teste., 68
Barb, James,
  leg., 66
Barb, Moses,
  will of, 66

Barb, Nancy E.,
  leg., 66
Barb, Peter,
  leg., 66
Barb, Peter B.,
  leg., 66
Bargerhoff, Abner,
  ex., 139
Bargerhoff, Clara P.,
  teste., 139
Bargerhoff, Jonas,
  will of, 139
Bargerhoff, Leticcia,
  leg., 139
Bargerhoff, Margaret,
  leg., 139
Bartlett, Eliza A.,
  leg., 161
Bartlett, Elizabeth F.,
  leg., 161
Bartlett, Ransdell,
  will of, 161
Bartlett, Rebecca H.,
  leg., 161
Bartlett, Susanna,
  leg., 161
Bartlett, Thomas N.,
  teste., 166
Bassel, Daniel,
  wife of, 83
Bassel, John,
  leg., 42
Bassel, Louisa,
  leg., 83
Bassell, Benjamin,
  teste., 110
Bastable, A. M.,
  teste., 22
  will of, 98
Bastable, Ann,
  note, 98
Bastable, George,
  teste., 16
Bastable, J. G.,
  note, 98
Bastable, Jane,
  ex., 98
  leg., 98
Bastable, May,
  ex., 138
  leg., 98, 138
Bastable, Milton W.,
  leg., 98

Name Index   (Bla-Bro)

Name Index   (Cla-Cri)

Name Index

Name Index   (Fit-Gor)

Name Index   (Har-Hin)

Hinkle, Mary Ann,
  leg., 142
Hinkle, Mary J.,
  leg., 140
Hinkle, Matilda,
  heirs of, 112
Hinkle, Melinda,
  leg., 19
Hinkle, Melvina,
  leg., 162
Hinkle, Minnie F.,
  leg., 140
Hinkle, Olive,
  ex., 155
  leg., 59, 155
Hinkle, Valentine,
  ex., 81
Hinkle, Valentine J.,
  teste., 63, 135
Hodges, Bushrod B.,
  leg., 82
Hodges, Elizabeth W.,
  ex., 82
  leg., 82
Hodges, George M.,
  leg., 82
Hodges, James F.,
  leg., 82
Hodges, John Henry,
  leg., 82
Hodges, John R.,
  will of, 82
Hodges, Malinda A.,
  leg., 82
Hodges, Melissa M.,
  leg., 92
Hodges, Mildred S.,
  leg., 82
Hodges, Oscar F.,
  leg., 82
Hodges, Theophelus F.,
  leg., 82
Hoff, John G.,
  teste., 161
Hollen, Elizabeth,
  leg., 136
Hollen, John A.,
  leg., 136
Hollen, Mary E.,
  leg., 136
Hollen, Wellington,
  will of, 136

Hollen, William F.,
  leg., 136
Hollen, Zebb D.,
  leg., 136
Hoofman, Amos,
  ex., 23
  leg., 23
Hoofman, Andrew,
  leg., 23
Hoofman, Anthony I.,
  ex., 23
  leg., 23
Hoofman, John,
  leg., 23
Hoofman, Joseph,
  will of, 23
Hoofman, Joseph Jr.,
  leg., 23
Hopkins, K.,
  ex., 17
Hosaflook, J.,
  lands of, 126
Houghton, Anna,
  leg., 70
Houser, Joseph,
  teste., 92
Howes, Cyntha Ann,
  leg., 14
Howes, Daniel,
  teste., 14
Howes, John,
  teste., 14
Hoy, John,
  land, 39
Huffman, D. P.,
  teste., 86
Huffman, Henry L.,
  will of, 86
Huffman, Henry T.,
  leg., 86
Huffman, Jane,
  leg., 86
Huffman, Joseph,
  teste., 147
Huffman, Polly,
  leg., 112
Huffman, Sampson,
  ex., 86
Huffman, Sedrick L.,
  leg., 86
Huffman, Susan,
  leg., 86

Name Index   (Hul-Jac)

Name Index

Name Index   (Kid-Lig)

Name Index   (Mar-Mea)

Meek, Nancy,
    leg., 21
Merrill, Rachel R.,
    leg., 110
Michael, Anne,
    leg., 23
Mick, Adam,
    leg., 119
Mick, Mary,
    will of, 119
Mick, Nicholas,
    leg., 119
Middleton, Henry C.,
    leg., 54
Middleton, Henry O.,
    estate of, 59
    ex., 95
    land, 4
    leg., 95
    will of, 54
Middleton, James E.,
    ex., 54
    leg., 54
Middleton, Julia A.,
    ex., 54
    leg., 54
Miles, Elizabeth,
    leg., 160
Miller, Daniel C.,
    teste., 66
Miller, Nancy,
    heirs of, 16
Miller, Rachel C.,
    leg., 4
Mills, Elizabeth D.,
    guardian for, 66
Mills, James,
    land of, 97
Mills, James E.,
    guardian for, 66
Mills, Mary,
    leg., 39
Mills, Mary J. C.,
    leg., 66
Mills, Peter,
    guardian for, 66
Mills, Virginia,
    leg., 66
Monday, N. G.,
    teste., 28
Moon, Nathaniel, Jr.,
    teste., 13

Moon, Nathaniel, Sr.,
    teste., 13
Moon, Schuyler P.,
    teste., 13
Moore, B. F.,
    teste., 161
Moore, Chesley K.,
    will of, 72
Moore, Eliza,
    leg., 72
Morgan, A. B.,
    heirs of, 47
Morgan, Amos B.,
    heirs of, 118
Morgan, Elizabeth,
    leg., 117, 118
Morgan, Grace H.,
    leg., 47, 117
Morgan, Harriet,
    leg., 47
Morgan, Hattie,
    ex., 118
    leg., 118
    will of, 117
Morgan, J. J.,
    commissioner, 160
    settlement with, 97
    teste., 97
Morgan, Jane,
    leg., 117
Morgan, Luceba,
    leg., 47, 117, 118
    teste., 118
Morgan, Lydia H.,
    leg., 47
Morgan, Lydia N.,
    will of, 118
Morgan, M. B.,
    widow of, 47
Morgan, Maria L.,
    leg., 47
Morgan, Mary Ann,
    leg., 117
Morgan, Maxwell W.,
    leg., 47, 118
Morgan, Milton W.,
    leg., 118
Morgan, Olive,
    leg., 117
Morgan, Theodore,
    will of, 47
Moss, John S.,
    leg., 165

UPSHUR COUNTY, WEST VIRGINIA

Name Index (Pau-Pos)

Paugh, William,
will of, 75
Perry, Emiline,
leg.,128
Perry, Harrick,
leg., 128
Perry, Hubbard B.,
will of, 128
Perry, Lucy J.,
leg., 128
Peters, L. L. D.,
teste., 96
Peterson, David T.,
teste., 98
Peterson, Lydia,
leg., 24
Phillips, Albert,
leg., 70
Phillips, Beecher W.,
teste., 111
Phillips, Burton,
leg., 70
Phillips, David,
leg., 70
Phillips, Electa,
leg., 70
Phillips, Estella,
leg., 97
Phillips, Esther,
leg., 14
Phillips, George,
land of, 97
leg., 70
Phillips, Grant,
leg., 70
Phillips, Horace,
wife of, 100
Phillips, Horace A.,
will of, 69
Phillips, John,
leg., 70
Phillips, Lynn,
ex., 128
teste., 128
Phillips, Milly R.,
leg., 147
Phillips, Simeon,
leg., 70
Phillips, Susan,
ex., 70
leg., 100

Phillips, Uriah,
land of, 70
Phipps, Daniel,
wife of, 41
Phipps, Elizabeth,
leg., 41
Phipps, George,
bond, 111
Phipps, Margaret,
leg., 111
Pinnell, Catherine,
leg., 104
Pinnell, D. S.,
teste., 7
Pinnell, David S.,
teste., 116
Pinnell, J. M.,
teste., 121
Pinnell, John M.,
ex., 104
Pinnell, Dr. P. F., (?)
ex., 121
Pinnell, P. F.,
teste., 22, 121
Pinnell, Philip F.,
teste., 93, 110
Post, Abraham,
will of, 10
Post, Abram,
ex., 10
leg., 10
teste., 19, 124
Post, Christina,
leg., 10
Post, Daniel,
ex., 10
will of, 134
Post, G. E.,
teste., 163
Post, George,
leg., 10
Post, Ira,
teste., 10
Post, Isaac,
leg., 10
Post, Jane,
leg., 134
Post, John,
loan, 85
Post, Mary,
leg., 67, 134

Name Index   (Pos-Reg)

Sexton, Almyra E.,
  leg., 76
Sexton, Amy A.,
  leg., 88
Sexton, Anne L.,
  leg., 76
Sexton, Augustus W.,
  will of, 76
Sexton, Freeman S.,
  leg., 76
Sexton, George A.,
  ex., 88
Sexton, James,
  land, 91
Sexton, Libby Gray,
  leg., 91
Sexton, Lucinda,
  will of, 91
Sexton, Mary Eva,
  leg., 91
Sexton, Rosa M.,
  leg., 91
Sexton, Sarah A.,
  leg., 88
Sexton, Sarah E.,
  leg., 88
Sexton, Virginia L.,
  leg., 89
Sexton, William,
  will of, 88
Sexton, William A.,
  note of, 88
Sexton, Worthington,
  leg., 76
Shackleford, Lucy C.,
  leg., 82
Sharpes, James M.,
  teste., 101
Shaver, John,
  will of, 160
Shaver, Rachael,
  leg., 160
Sheets, Malinda,
  leg., 112
Shobe, Hannah M.,
  leg., 125
Shobe, John,
  teste., 11
Shreve, Benjamine F. H.,
  ex., 145
  leg., 145
Shreve, Chas. B.,
  teste., 73

Shreve, Granville T.,
  teste., 73
Shreve, J. B.,
  teste., 1, 73
Shreve, John B.,
  land, 4
  teste., 4
Shreve, M. E.,
  teste., 148
Shreve, Marian H.,
  leg., 145
Shreve, Sarah M.,
  leg., 145
Shreves, Martin E.,
  teste., 74
Shumaker, D. H.,
  teste., 12
Silcott, Louisa E.,
  leg., 76
Simin, John D.,
  ex., 5
Simmons, Ruhannah,
  leg., 3
Simon, Elias,
  will of, 107
Simon, J. B.,
  teste., 107
Simon, John B.,
  ex., 107
Simon, Leonard R.,
  ex., 107
  leg., 107
Simon, Nancy,
  leg., 107
Simons, Elizath M.,
  leg., 87
Simpson, Allen A.,
  teste., 164
Simpson, Henry,
  ex., 35
  teste., 83
Sims, Sarah S.,
  leg., 2
Siron, Henry F.,
  leg., 125
Siron, John B.,
  leg., 125
Siron, Joseph,
  leg., 125
Siron, Lydia S.,
  leg., 125
Siron, Magdalene S.,
  leg., 125

Siron, Valentine,
  will of, 125
Siron, Valentine B.,
  ex., 125
  leg., 125
Siron, William W.,
  leg., 125
Slaughter, James E.,
  teste., 7
Smallridge, Charlotte,
  leg., 111
Smallridge, Jacob J.,
  leg., 111
Smallridge, Samuel D.,
  leg., 111
Smallridge, William,
  will of, 111
Smallridge, William B.,
  leg., 111
Smith, Abram A.,
  teste., 56
Smith, Bersheba N.,
  leg., 102
Smith, Christain,
  will of, 93
Smith, Esther T.,
  leg., 102
Smith, J. L. B.,
  will of, 102
Smith, James L.,
  teste., 133
Smith, Jane,
  leg., 93
Smith, John,
  teste., 55
Smith, Joseph C.,
  leg., 93
Smith, Lucinda,
  leg., 85
Smith, Margaret,
  leg., 24
Smith, Martin J.,
  wife of, 24
Smith, Mary E.,
  leg., 131
Smith, Perry D.,
  leg., 93
Smith, Pricilla,
  heirs of, 111
Smith, Prudy,
  leg., 164

Smith, Virginia,
  leg., 131
  will of, 148
Smith, William,
  leg., 148
Snell, Biny E.,
  leg., 157
Snyder, Ephram,
  teste., 162
Spore, Louisa,
  leg., 146
Squire, Olen B.,
  leg., 83
Starcher, Elvira,
  teste., 96
Starcher, Jacob,
  teste., 96
Stansberry, Celia,
  leg., 130
Stansberry, Elizah,
  contract, 94
  teste., 94
Starn, George W.,
  teste., 130
Stewart, George W.,
  teste., 99
Stout, Benjamin,
  leg., 42
  will of, 42
Stout, Daniel,
  log., 42
Stout, Deborah,
  leg., 42, 96
Stout, George,
  leg., 42
Stout, Hezekiah,
  leg., 42
Stout, John,
  leg., 42
Stout, Martha,
  leg., 42
Strader, Abram,
  lands of, 65
  teste., 36, 140
Strader, Asa,
  teste., 127
Strader, G.,
  teste., 78
Strader, Granville,
  ex., 78
Strader, Jacob,
  land, 31

Name Index

Strader, Jacob B.,
 contract, 7
Strader, James A.,
 teste., 137
Strader, John,
 land of, 24
Strader, Jonas
 will of, 7
Strader, Mary,
 leg., 165
Strader, Valentine,
 ex., 7
 teste., 72, 88
Stratton, James N.,
 teste., 145
Summerville, E. T.,
 advisor, 30
 teste., 30
Swecker, Barbara,
 leg., 10
Swecker, Daniel,
 wife of, 10
Swick, A. S.,
 teste., 143
Swisher, Sarah,
 leg., 23

Talbott, (see also
 Tolbert)
Talbott, John S.,
 teste., 163
Tallman, Benny,
 will of, 79
Tallman, Cyrus G.,
 leg., 79
Tallman, Luella,
 leg., 79
Tallman, Nancy E.,
 leg., 79
Tallman, Sophronia,
 ex., 79
 leg., 79
Teets, Ethelinda,
 heirs of, 140
Teets, J. A.,
 teste., 154
Teets, Lavina,
 leg., 140
Teets, Margaret,
 leg., 140
Teets, Naomi,
 leg., 140

Tenney, Addison,
 wife of, 41
Tenney, Cerene Ann,
 leg., 41
Tenney, Daniel,
 leg., 165
Tenney, G. W.,
 teste., 87
Tenney, George A.,
 leg., 80
Tenney, George W.,
 leg., 66
Tenney, Hannah I.,
 leg., 147
Tenney, John L.,
 heirs of, 41
Tenney, Jonathan,
 land, 80
Tenney, Josiah,
 leg., 41
Tenney, Labany,
 leg., 80
Tenney, Lyda,
 will of, 41
Tenney, Lyia,
 land, 29
Tenney, Ocadevier,
 leg., 29
Tenney, Peter,
 land of, 41
Tenney, Peter Jr.,
 leg., 80
Tenney, Peter Sr.,
 will of, 80
Tenney, Philo,
 will of, 109
Tenney, Rebecca,
 leg., 109
Tenney, Sandusky,
 leg., 80
Tenney, Sarah Catherine,
 leg., 80
Teter, J.,
 teste., 60
Teter, John,
 land, 106
Teter, Katharine,
 leg., 77
Thompson, Andrew Jr.,
 leg., 35
Thompson, Andrew Sr.,
 will of, 35

Thompson, Catherine,
  leg., 35
Thrash, David H.,
  leg., 163
Thrash, H. J.,
  will of, 163
Thrash, Melissa J.,
  leg., 163
Thrash, Michael,
  leg., 163
Tolbert, David J.,
  ex., 24, 96
  leg., 24
Tolbert, George M.,
  ex., 24
  leg., 24
Tolbert, Perry,
  teste., 160
Tolbert, Samuel T.,
  will of, 24
Toney, Robert,
  leg., 127
Totten, W. G. L.,
  teste., 89, 138
Townsend, R. H.,
  teste., 24, 45, 58
Townsend, Rebecca,
  leg., 71
Townsent, Ezekiel,
  ex., 11
Townsent, Wm.,
  ex., 11
Trask, William,
  leg., 18

Vincent, Hezekiah,
  leg., 21
Vincent, I. W.,
  teste., 131
Vincent, John,
  leg., 21
Vincent, John Sr.,
  will of, 21
Vincent, Lydia Y.,
  leg., 137
Vincent, Sarah,
  leg., 21
Vincent, W.,
  leg., 21

Wade, J. O.,
  teste., 69
Walden, John,
  vs. Alexander Ireland, 49
Walsh, Michael,
  teste., 103
Wamsley, N. B.,
  teste., 25, 27, 29, 59,
  65, 80
Wamsley, Noah B.,
  advisor, 25
  teste., 79, 80
Ward, C. S.,
  leg., 162
Ward, Jackson,
  leg., 121
  will of, 143
Ward, Jesse C.,
  leg., 162
Ward, Job,
  leg., 121
Ward, John,
  leg., 162
Ward, John W.,
  leg., 143
  will of, 158
Ward, Joseph,
  teste., 52, 99
  will of, 121
Ward, Kinsey,
  will of, 162
Ward, Letcher,
  leg., 162
Ward, Martin V.,
  leg., 162
Ward, Nelson R.,
  leg., 162
Ward, Rebecca,
  leg., 121
Ward, Sophia A.,
  leg., 162
Ward, Vashti,
  leg., 143
Ward, Walter,
  teste., 145
Ward, Willis O. B.,
  ex., 162
  leg., 162
Warner, George,
  teste., 114

Windell, J. W.,
  teste., 131
Windell, James M.,
  teste., 146
Windle, James W.,
  teste., 60
Wood, Joseph,
  will of, 1
Woodley, A. Virginia,
  will of, 149
Woodley, E. E. H.,
  teste., 149
Woodley, Elizabeth H. H.,
  leg., 149
Woodley, Willis H.,
  leg., 149
Woodley, Willis H. Jr.,
  leg., 149
Woods, Jemina,
  leg., 69
Woods, Joshua,
  ex., 69
Woods, Mary,
  heirs of, 16
Wyrick, Mary S. M. Rosa,
  leg., 4

Yeates, Louisa S.,
  leg., 57
Yoakem, Edwin S. D.,
  ex., 166
  leg., 166
Yoakem, George W.,
  leg., 166
Yoakem, James M.,
  leg., 166

Yoakem, Jane,
  leg., 166
Yoakem, John,
  will of, 166
Yoakem, Noah,
  leg., 166
Yoakem, Sarah A.,
  leg., 166
Young, Ammylis,
  leg., 97
Young, Anson,
  teste., 14
Young, Earl E.,
  teste., 26
  will of, 101
Young, Festus,
  settlement with, 97
  teste., 70, 97, 111, 120
Young, Gilbert,
  will of, 97
Young, James,
  leg., 122
Young, Loyal,
  teste., 76
Young, M. P.,
  teste., 76
Young, Mary E.,
  leg., 101
Young, Nancy,
  teste., 120
Young, Nancy A.,
  leg., 107
Young, Pascal P.,
  teste., 3
Youts, Catherine,
  leg., 16

* * *

www.ingramcontent.com/pod-product-compliance
Lightning Source LLC
LaVergne TN
LVHW091202080426
835509LV00006B/784